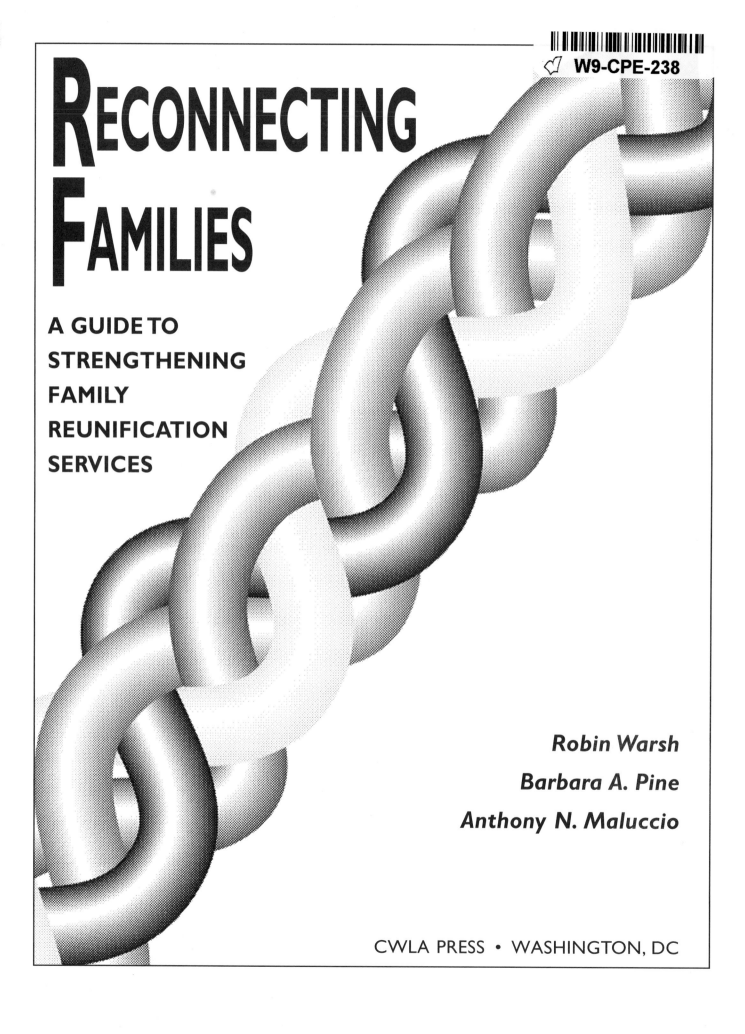

RECONNECTING FAMILIES

A GUIDE TO STRENGTHENING FAMILY REUNIFICATION SERVICES

Robin Warsh

Barbara A. Pine

Anthony N. Maluccio

CWLA PRESS • WASHINGTON, DC

CWLA Press is an imprint of the Child Welfare League of America.

© 1996 by the Child Welfare League of America, Inc. All rights reserved. Neither this book nor any part may be reproduced or transmitted in any form or by any means, electronic or mechanical, including photocopying, microfilming, and recording, or by any information storage and retrieval system, without permission in writing from the publisher, with the following exception: permission is granted to the purchaser of this publication to reproduce the materials in the Additional Forms section of the *Guide* and the materials that comprise the *Resource Workbook*. Such copies shall be used solely as part of the implementation of the Family Reunification Project and are not to be resold or otherwise distributed.

For information on this or other CWLA publications, contact the CWLA Publications Department at the address below.

CHILD WELFARE LEAGUE OF AMERICA, INC.
440 First Street, NW, Suite 310, Washington, DC 20001-2085

CURRENT PRINTING (last digit)
10 9 8 7 6 5 4 3 2 1

Cover and text design by Jennifer R. Geanakos

Printed in the United States of America

ISBN # 0–87868–574–X

CONTENTS

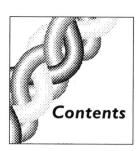

Contents

"If we keep thinking we're doing it right, we're never going to improve."

—*A Social Worker*

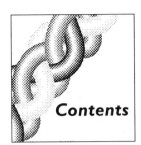

Contents

FOREWORD

An Open Letter to Agency Directors from the
Connecticut Department of Children and Families

In January 1993, Robin Warsh, Barbara Pine, and Anthony Maluccio approached the Connecticut Department of Children and Families (DCF) with an exciting offer—that DCF participate with them in a pilot project to assess family reunification efforts. They had drafted an assessment tool—this *Guide*—to help child welfare agencies evaluate and improve their family reunification services and needed a field test site for the project. The project involved selecting DCF staff members to participate in a work team to assess our family reunification service delivery system and to make recommendations in regard to policy, program, training, and resources.

The offer was timely for many reasons. First, DCF had just begun to clarify its mission, to strengthen its commitment to families, and to renew its goal of serving children in their own homes. Second, DCF had just undergone a symbolic but important name change from the Department of Children and Youth Services to the Department of Children and Families. Third, DCF was planning to expand its family reunification services. The opportunity to use their tool, *Reconnecting Families: A Guide to Strengthening Family Reunification Services,* to assess our current practices and identify areas requiring improvement was most welcome and we eagerly joined the project.

Time has indicated that this was indeed a wise decision, one that has been of enormous benefit both to DCF and to the families it serves. The most tangible outcome has been a set of 65 recommendations for improving DCF's family reunification service delivery system. These recommendations were developed by our staff as they used the *Guide* to review the roles and responsibilities of our staff, of foster parents, and of provider agencies; evaluate our preparation of children and our model for visiting; and examine our relationship with other systems such as the courts and schools. The recommendations are creative, founded in sound social work practice, and most importantly, practical. We have been extremely impressed with the quality of the work teams, their positive attitude, their dedication to families and children, and the clarity and helpfulness of their work product.

DCF has since begun implementing the recommendations. For example, we have prepared an information packet that is given to families at the time a child is placed. The packet includes an explanation of the reunification process, the family's rights and responsibilities, DCF's responsibilities and roles, and key information about social workers, attorneys, and other community providers assisting the family.

Foreword

Additional and unplanned benefits have ensued for both DCF and the families we serve as a result of our undertaking the Family Reunification Project:

- Use of the *Guide* has resulted in an intense focus by DCF on the needs of children and families separated by placement. This focus alone produced increased staff competency in family reunification and a renewed belief in the importance of family.

- The *Guide* empowered staff members and is still encouraging them to evaluate and recommend methods of improving our service delivery system.

- Use of the *Guide* exposed us to a model for planning change that we may apply to other components of our service delivery system.

- The *Guide* was a valuable resource in helping DCF respond to the requirements of new federal legislation in regard to the provision of family preservation and family support services.

The Department of Children and Families has gained much from its participation in the Family Reunification Project. More important, I believe families have been well-served when we have followed the strategies outlined in the *Guide*. I encourage you to commit your agencies to using this important tool to assess and improve your family reunification services.

SHARON MARTIN
Deputy Commissioner
Connecticut Department of Children and Families

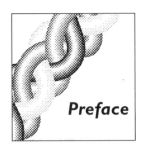

Whether or not to reunite children in out-of-home care with their families of origin is one of the most complicated decisions that child welfare practitioners face. Difficult questions loom: How do we both preserve families and protect children from harm? What constitutes "good-enough" parenting? How do we weigh the risk of returning children to their families against the risk of prolonging their stay in out-of-home care? Moreover, once the reunification decision has been made by all involved, how do we implement it well?

In response to these questions, public as well as private child welfare agencies have been reexamining their family reunification policies and services. Accordingly, this book, *Reconnecting Families: A Guide to Strengthening Family Reunification Services,* and its *Resource Workbook* are designed to help agencies assess and improve their service delivery system so as to reunite children and their families effectively and promptly.

The *Guide* builds on our work for over a decade in a variety of projects that have laid the foundation for a comprehensive approach to service delivery in family reunification. These include five federally funded grants, carried out in collaboration with all six state child welfare agencies in New England and with selected schools of social work. The grants involved in-service training of social workers and foster parents, social work practice with biological parents, and education of social workers for child welfare.

In regard to family reunification, a previous project of ours (carried out from 1988 to 1990) had produced a series of publications and training materials to enhance the knowledge and skills of social workers, foster parents, child care personnel, and others in the practice of family reunification. Since 1991, we have built on these materials as we developed, field tested, and disseminated the *Guide*.

Reconnecting Families: A Guide to Strengthening Family Reunification Services is firmly grounded in the reality of child welfare practice today, as it was developed and refined in an extensive field testing process that actively involved child welfare practitioners and administrators. The *Guide* addresses agency personnel at all levels—from administrators to line staff members—who are responsible for planning and implementing family reunification services.

The *Guide* is also a teaching tool. It contains current thinking on the principles and strategies that promote sound family reunification policies, programs, and practices. It is also, as we learned in its field testing, a powerful tool for unleashing creativity and teamwork among staff members. The process of self-assessment and change that the *Guide* facilitates conveys a new approach to shaping a responsive child welfare system, one that is shared by staff members at all levels. We hope that the *Guide* will prove useful to you in examining and strengthening the range of services your agency provides to children and their families.

ACKNOWLEDGMENTS

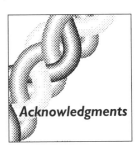

Just as the practice of family reunification requires the work of many individuals, each of whom contributes essential expertise, support, and insight, so too has this publication relied on the involvement of many people.

For their generosity and sustained commitment to supporting our efforts to improve child welfare service delivery, we thank The Annie E. Casey Foundation and its staff—Douglas Nelson, Executive Director; Kathleen Feely, Associate Director; and John Mattingly, Senior Associate.

We are grateful to June Gary Hopps, Dean, Boston College Graduate School of Social Work, for her support. We deeply appreciate her continuing encouragement, guidance, and interest in our work.

We thank the members of our Project Advisory Group, each of whom provided invaluable guidance on the development of this volume by helping to ensure its relevance to agency practice. They are:

- Ray Barrett, New Hampshire Division for Children and Youth Services;

- Lynn Boyle, Vermont Social and Rehabilitative Services/Social Services;

- Beverly Burke, Connecticut Department of Children and Families;

- Patty Casey, Massachusetts Department of Social Services;

- Carolyn Cocklyn, New Hampshire Division for Children and Youth Services;

- Tom Driane, New Hampshire Division for Children and Youth Services;

- Edith Fein, Casey Family Services (Hartford, CT);

- Freda Plumley, Maine Department of Child and Family Services; and

- Bruce Rollins, Rhode Island Department of Children, Youth and Families.

We have had the good fortune of working with a range of experts on family reunification, each of whom responded to earlier drafts of this material. We are grateful for their pertinent questions, clarifying comments, and specific suggestions. They are:

- Mustafa Abdul-Salaam, New Haven Family Alliance;

- Ira Barbell, The Annie E. Casey Foundation;

- Paul Berkowitz, Massachusetts Department of Social Services;

- James Carr, Connecticut Department of Children and Families;

- Laura Downs, The Annie E. Casey Foundation;

- Joy Duva, Casey Family Services (Shelton, CT);

- Gail Foloran, Indiana University School of Social Work;

Acknowledgments

- Lauren Frey (formerly with Special Adoption Family Services), Massachusetts Families for Kids;

- Ray Hall, New Haven Family Alliance;

- Mark Hardin, Center on Children and the Law, American Bar Association;

- Peg Hess, Columbia University School of Social Work;

- Patrick Johnson, Catholic Family Services (Hartford, CT);

- Sara Kobylenski, Casey Family Services (Vermont);

- Robert Lewis, Special Adoption Family Services;

- Carmen Martinez, Milford Mental Health Center;

- Ann Mikulak, Connecticut Department of Children and Families;

- Steve Nagler, Yale Child Study Center;

- Leah O'Leary, Boston College Graduate School of Social Work;

- Eileen Mayers Pasztor, Child Welfare League of America;

- Jestina Richardson, United Homes for Children;

- Greg Sorozan, Massachusetts Department of Social Services;

- Dorothy Weitzman, Boston College Graduate School of Social Work; and

- Jeanne Zamosky, Familystrength.

We owe a special debt of gratitude to the Connecticut Department of Children and Families (DCF), former DCF Commissioner Rose Alma Senatore, and DCF Deputy Commissioner Sharon Martin, for agreeing to have DCF serve as the field test site for the *Guide*. Throughout the field test, DCF held fast to its commitment to the philosophy of family preservation, to the value of self-assessment leading to system change, and to the provision of the resources needed to carry out our work.

We also thank the participants in the field test: the members of the Implementation Team, Work Teams, outside experts who joined the Work Teams, and invited guests to the final Planning for Change Meeting. Their innovative ideas, positive attitude toward change, and commitment to vulnerable children and their families make for a stronger Department of Children and Families and a more useful and pertinent *Guide*:

- Implementation Team—Jim Carr, Marisa Giarnella-Porco, Tom Gilman, Bill Howe, Susan Kintner, Sharon Martin, and Carole Porto;

- Work Team (Hamden)—Susan Kintner (Coordinator), Tom Buch, Judy Burger-Gossart, Sandy Corcoran, Arlene Esposito, Star Gilliams, Jeanne Holm, Carmen Martinez, Vicki Maury, Vinita Parker, Barbara Stark, Bernie Ulusky, and Rose Zanders;

- Work Team (Willimantic)—Marisa Giarnella-Porco (Coordinator), Beverly Burke, Maureen Chmelicki, Herb Donahue, Helen Hopson, George Kozcon, Audrey Marino, Mark Mathieu, Charlotte May, Kim Meldrum, Edma Perez, Ann Quinn, Bonnie Resnick, Fernando Rausch, Sherry Rautenberg, Sandra Rudin, Dianne Sinapi, Maria Tatis, and Lisa Terpening;

- Outside Experts—Richard Aldridge, Leona Ambrosini, Paul Bakulski, Audrey Burke, Lois Earles, Marylou Giovanucci, Linnea Loin, Sherman Malone, Janet Murphy, and Pat Weel; and

Acknowledgments

- Planning for Change Meeting (Guests)—Gary Blau, David Brumer, Ray Farrington, Robert Kramer, Sharon Martin, John Mattingly, Susan O'Brien, Rita Pelaggi, Maryann Poinelli, Andrea Routh, June Roy, and Rose Alma Senatore (former DCF Commissioner).

We also wish to express our thanks to the staff of the Children's Bureau, Region I, U.S. Department of Health and Human Services, and especially to Tina Janey-Burrell, Program Manager, and Linda Mitchell, Program Specialist. Their quick recognition of the potential value of the *Guide*, and their readiness to create avenues to help support its use, have been very important to us. They are colleagues in every sense of the word.

We gratefully acknowledge the hard work of Lisa Driscoll, a social work student whom each of us has had the pleasure of teaching, who reviewed and abstracted many of the resources that appear in Part 4 of this volume. She brought to the task her rich practice wisdom and a zeal for knowledge. We wish her the best in what we know will be a distinguished career in child welfare.

Once again, as we have for nearly a decade, we thank Pamela Harrison, our secretary, for her continued commitment to excellence. Especially now, while each of us has offices quite a distance from the others, coordination and communication are key. Pam is our center and we appreciate her enormously.

The challenges of family preservation require new solutions. We have been fortunate to have the collaboration of so many forward-thinking and creative professionals as we work toward changed service delivery, and look forward to continued work together.

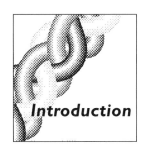

The increase in attention that family reunification services are receiving is part of the revolution in child welfare services that has been taking place in the last two decades in the United States. This revolution was spurred by passage of the Adoption Assistance and Child Welfare Act of 1980 (P.L. 96–272), which codified the need for placement prevention and reunification services into federal law. The rapid development of family preservation services to prevent unnecessary out-of-home placement has been a major feature of the revolutionary changes taking place. To date, however, much less attention has been paid to services that help to reunite families after placement has occurred.

Although comprehensive national data are not available, most children in out-of-home care do return home. In 1990, 67% of the 202,000 children who left out-of-home care were either reunited with their families or placed with relatives.* Large numbers of those who return home, however, eventually reenter care. Wulczyn** found a 22% reentry rate for children reunited with their families in New York State, and Goerge† reported a 33% reentry rate for families reunited in Illinois. These numbers were a major force behind our work on *Reconnecting Families: A Guide to Strengthening Family Reunification Services*, as they suggest an urgent need to improve services that help families to reunite and remain together.

How the *Guide* Was Developed

The seeds for the *Guide* were planted between 1988 and 1990, when the authors carried out a family reunification training and demonstration project with funding from The Annie E. Casey Foundation and the U.S. Department of Health and Human Services. The project developed and disseminated a variety of training materials and reports that identified fundamental family reunification policies, concepts, program components, practice strategies, and social work competencies.

In 1991, with a planning grant from The Annie E. Casey Foundation, we began developing a comprehensive proposal for improving the capacity of child welfare agencies to deliver family reunification services. In collaboration with an advisory group of child welfare agency staff and with consultation from national experts, we described the components of a comprehensive service delivery system for family reunification. The planning grant helped us to clarify the need to develop this description into an assessment and planning tool if agencies were to effectively carry out the system change required for an improved service delivery system.

---

*   T. Tatara, *Characteristics of children in substitute and adoptive care: A statistical summary of the VCIS National Child Welfare Data Base—Based on FY 82 through FY 90 data* (Washington, DC: American Public Welfare Association, 1993).

** F. Wulczyn, Caseload dynamics and foster care reentry, *Social Service Review, 65* (1991): 133–156.

†   R. M. Goerge, The reunification process in substitute care, *Social Service Review, 64* (1990): 422–457.

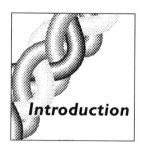

Introduction

The need for such a tool led to our current project and the publication of this *Guide*. In 1992, we received a two-year grant from The Annie E. Casey Foundation to develop, field test, refine, and publish a self-study manual to help agencies evaluate and strengthen their family reunification service delivery systems. By the end of the first year we had developed a draft of the assessment tool and a preliminary set of resource materials. Still needed, however, was a method for agencies to use in carrying out the assessment and change process.

Convinced that system change must occur from the bottom up, as well as from the top down, we created an approach that involved staff members at all levels of the agency who, through group discussion and decision making, would be able to examine their own practice and agency supports and recommend improvements. To see if the approach worked, we turned to the Connecticut Department of Children and Families (DCF) to conduct a comprehensive field test of the *Guide*. During the spring and summer of 1993, we observed the DCF staff as they used the *Guide*, asking questions and refining the process of using the *Guide* as we learned from their experiences. The results of the field test form the basis of the material contained in Part 2 of the *Guide*, "Carrying Out the Family Reunification Project." The experiences of the participants, captured in their quotes, appear throughout.

As its developmental history shows, the *Guide* is well-grounded in practice. Its contents and process reflect the contributions of national experts, many of whom are child welfare administrators and practitioners, as well as the results of extensive field testing. As with any guide to system change, it will require adaptation by each agency that uses it. We welcome the opportunity to hear about your experiences with it.

Purposes and Benefits of Using the *Guide*

Reconnecting Families: A Guide to Strengthening Family Reunification Services provides you and your agency with the guidance you need to conduct what we call the Family Reunification Project, that is, to comprehensively assess the policies, programs, practices, and resources now in place in your agency to help reunify children in family foster care with their families.* Through the *Guide*, the Family Reunification Project helps you to evaluate your agency's relationships with other parts of the service delivery system, particularly the courts, community provider agencies, and schools. Completion of the Family Reunification Project provides you with a full picture of the strengths and weaknesses of all components of your agency's family reunification service delivery system, as well as a plan for improving that system.

For a number of reasons, the self-assessment process that underpins the project is as important as the results it produces. First, as a tool for self-assessment, the *Guide* calls for an open discussion of agency strengths and needs by the staff members who actually plan and implement family reunification services. This is no audit by outside experts, no judgment by people who do not walk in your shoes.

Second, the project is carried out by staff members from all levels of the agency—including policymakers, managers, supervisors, trainers, social workers,

---

* The *Guide* focuses on children placed in family foster care rather than those placed in kinship care. In our view, the latter group represents a different phenomenon, with its own unique features and strategies—and one deserving of separate, extended consideration. Furthermore, although much of what is covered can apply to children placed in group care or residential care settings, the *Guide* is organized primarily for assessing family reunification and nonrelative family foster care services.

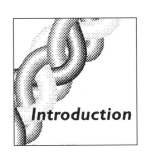

foster parents, attorneys, and staff members from community agencies—as well as by biological parents. The project brings together the full range of players involved in family reunification work to consider current practices and problems. The process of shared problem-solving can result in a "we're in this together" attitude, as people at all levels in the system are reminded of how complex family reunification work is, how difficult it is to create and maintain a responsive child welfare system, and how every person plays a vital part in shaping services.

Third, the *Guide* is a teaching tool. Because we have been working together for over eight years and with others around the country to develop family reunification materials, the *Guide* contains information on the current best thinking about family reunification policy and practice. Participants in the assessment process thus gain exposure to a wealth of practice strategies and approaches.

Fourth, in field testing, participants received a tremendous morale and creativity boost. Involvement in the assessment and planning process provides staff members and others with the opportunity to reflect on their work and consider, in lively exchanges with their coworkers, new and better ways to meet the needs of families. The process also produces a sense of optimism that improvements can, in fact, be made. Optimistic and empowered staff members are better able to foster these qualities in the families they serve.

Finally, the project's model of self-assessment and planning for system change in family reunification featured here is one that can be adapted to evaluate other programs and services in your agency.

What the *Guide* Contains

The *Guide* contains all of the materials needed to undertake the Family Reunification Project, with the exception of copies of various recommended readings and resources. It is organized into seven major parts and an Appendix.

Part 1: Overview of Family Reunification

Part 1 sets forth a redefinition of family reunification and a set of principles or beliefs about practice and policy that serve as the foundation for a system assessment and change process.

Part 2: Carrying Out the Family Reunification Project

Part 2 contains step-by-step instructions, materials, and helpful tips for carrying out the Family Reunification Project (the actual assessment and planning process). It is organized into six steps: Step One—Committing to the Project; Step Two—Forming the Teams; Step Three—Launching the Project; Step Four—Conducting the Assessment; Step Five—Planning for Change; and Step Six—Evaluating the Family Reunification Project.

Part 3: Framework for Assessment of Strengths and Needs

Part 3 contains 25 family reunification system components, organized into three sections that correspond with the three major contexts of the system: the child welfare agency as an organization, the agency's family reunification services, and the agency's relationships with other key organizations and systems. A brief definition of each component is followed by a list of "Key Elements for Success," which represent standards of best practice. Users are guided through the assessment process for each component with a set of worksheets and recommended readings and resources.

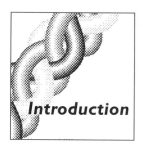

Introduction

Part 4: Annotated Bibliography

Part 4 contains an annotated bibliography to assist you as you conduct the Family Reunification Project and make needed improvements in your family reunification services. The abstracts of articles and books are organized into the following sections: (I) Family Reunification (General); (II) Improving Work and Workplaces; (III) Program Monitoring and Evaluation; (IV) Enhancing Cultural Competence; (V) Staff Development and Training; (VI) Working with the Legal System; (VII) Funding Services and Programs; and (VIII) Working with Children and Families.

Part 5: Resources

Part 5 contains selected guidelines and forms to help you conduct the self-assessment and make needed improvements in your family reunification services. These resources are organized into three sections: (I) Enhancing Cultural Competence; (II) Funding Services and Programs; and (III) Working with Children and Families.

Part 6: Selected Bibliography on Family Reunification After Foster Care

The readings listed in Part 6 supplement the annotated list provided in Part 4 and will be helpful in your efforts to improve your family reunification services.

Part 7: Additional Forms

Forms needed to complete the Family Reunification Project are provided for photocopying as needed.

Appendix: The Resource Workbook

The Appendix to the *Guide* contains the introduction, and other materials for the *Reconnecting Families Resource Workbook* and directions for photocopying and assembling *Resource Workbooks* for the various members of the teams. Each team member should receive a copy of the complete *Resource Workbook* at the outset of the Family Reunification Project. Bound copies of the *Resource Workbook* are available and may be ordered using the form at the end of the *Guide*.

PART I

OVERVIEW OF FAMILY REUNIFICATION

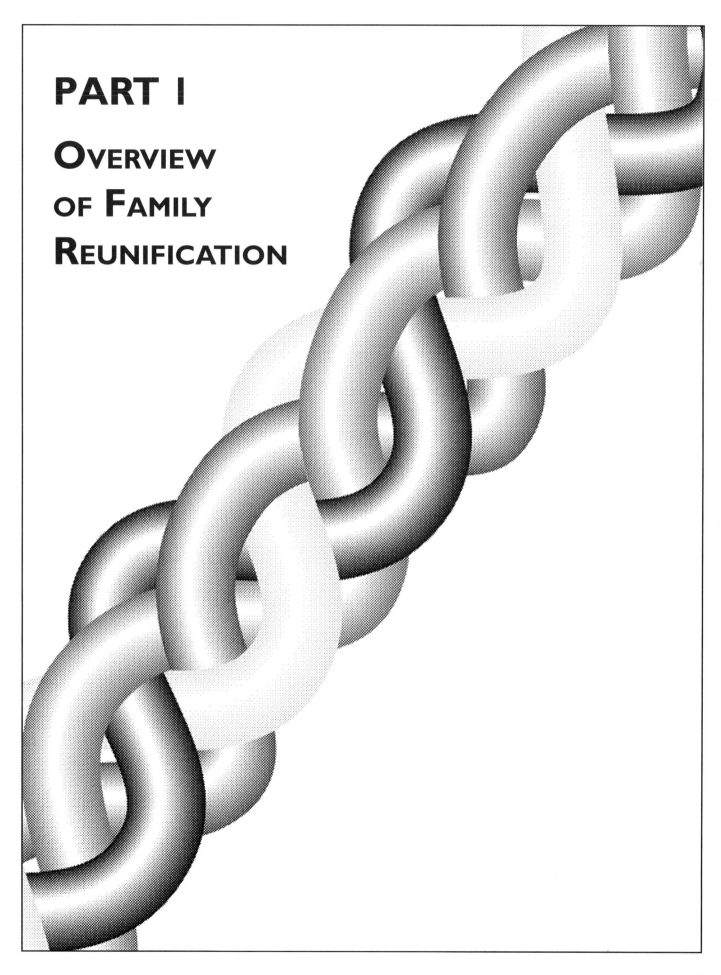

OVERVIEW OF FAMILY REUNIFICATION

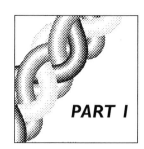

Since the beginning of the permanency planning revolution in child welfare in the 1970s and 1980s, family reunification practice has been based on the premise that children in out-of-home care should either be returned to their families of origin as quickly as possible or placed in another permanent family. This either-or orientation has long been supported—and in some ways required—by policy and law. For example, termination of parental rights has at times been sought inappropriately in cases where there are reasons to continue the parent-child relationship. Long-term family foster care has been rejected as a legitimate permanent plan even though some children find permanence when these relationships are stable. Thus, in the ground swell of support for permanency for children and the reforms accompanying it, the needs and interests of some families and children have been denied.

There are many parents who love their children and want to nurture them, but are unable to be full-time caregivers. The child welfare system's response to these parents has often been to test them beyond their limits by returning their children home, or to terminate their parental rights and forever sever their family bonds.

An Expanded Definition of Family Reunification

This either-or orientation is too simplistic and not in the best interests of the child. In its place, a family reunification orientation is needed that embodies a flexible approach to working with children in out-of-home care and their families—an approach that recognizes and meets children's and families' individual needs. This rethinking of family reunification has led to the development of the following expanded definition:

> Family reunification *is the planned process of reconnecting children in out-of-home care with their families by means of a variety of services and supports to the children, their families, and their foster parents or other service providers. It aims to help each child and family to achieve and maintain, at any given time, their optimal level of reconnection—from full reentry of the child into the family system to other forms of contact, such as visiting, that affirm the child's membership in the family.**

This expanded definition views family reunification as a dynamic process based on each child's and family's changing qualities, needs, and potential. With the right combination of services and supports, most families can get back

---

* A. N. Maluccio, R. Warsh, & B. A. Pine, Family reunification: An overview, in B. A. Pine, R. Warsh, and A. N. Maluccio (Eds.), *Together again: Family reunification in foster care* (Washington, DC: Child Welfare League of America, 1993), p. 6.

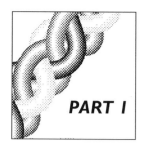

PART I

together. In those few situations where a relationship is neither possible nor desirable and termination of parental rights is warranted, children can be helped to move into new permanent families with some tangible link to their past in the form of pictures, a lifebook, or other family memorabilia.

The Principles of Family Reunification

This expanded definition of family reunification leads to the following principles, which form an important foundation for the development of sound policies, programs, and practices in family reunification:

A. With its emphasis on ensuring continuity of relationships and care for children, family reunification is an integral part of the philosophy of permanency planning.

B. Children are best reared in families, preferably their own; most families can care for their own children if properly assisted.

C. Family reunification practice must be guided by an ecologically oriented, competence-centered perspective, that emphasizes:

- promoting family empowerment,

- engaging in advocacy and social action,

- reaching for—and building on—family strengths,

- involving any and all whom the child considers family as partners, and

- providing needed services and supports.

D. Teamwork among the many parties involved in family reunification is critical.

E. All forms of human diversity—ethnic, racial, cultural, religious, life-style— as well as physical and mental challenges, must be respected.

F. A commitment to early and consistent child-family visiting is an essential ingredient in preparing for—and maintaining—reunification.

G. Foster parents and child care workers must be involved as members of the service delivery team. The agency should share information with them about the child and family that is shared with other service providers, involve them in decisions, and provide them with adequate training.

H. Many families will have continuing service needs in multiple areas. Services to meet these needs must be provided for as long as children and families require them to maintain the reunification.

I. Agencies must empower their staffs by providing adequate training and supervision and by using a team approach in making case decisions.

PART 2

CARRYING OUT THE FAMILY REUNIFICATION PROJECT

Step One:
Committing to the Project

Step Two:
Forming the Teams

Step Three:
Launching the Project

Step Four:
Conducting the Assessment

Step Five:
Planning for Change

Step Six:
Evaluating the Family Reunification Project

STEP ONE
COMMITTING TO THE PROJECT

Understanding the Project's Purposes and Process

Deciding to Undertake the Project

Publicizing the Project

RESPONSIBILITY

The Commissioner or Director, in consultation with other senior-level managers.

SUMMARY

Before you proceed further, you must decide whether or not your agency will undertake the Family Reunification Project. To help you make your decision, STEP ONE presents the Project's purposes and process; a description of the staffing required to carry it out; an activity that will help you weigh expected benefits against any concerns you have about the Project; and, should you decide to go ahead, ideas for publicizing the Project and gaining full advantage from your decision.

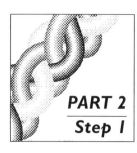
UNDERSTANDING THE PROJECT'S
PURPOSES AND PROCESS

Purpose

The Family Reunification Project can help you and your agency to conduct a self-assessment of the strengths and weaknesses of your family reunification system and develop an action plan for positive system change.

Process

Part 3 of the *Guide* identifies the 25 major components of a family reunification service delivery system, and the Key Elements for Success, or standards of best practice, for each. A Work Team comprising staff from all levels of your agency (see below) will review the Key Elements, decide whether each is a strength or weakness in your agency, and recommend plans for improvement where needed.

For example, *Component # 15: Visiting* identifies 17 Key Elements for Success that, when carried out, help ensure that visits are used as a tool to fully promote family reunification. One Key Element states that:

> *Children are returned home only after they have safely had unsupervised visits in their own home, including overnight visits and visits lasting several days or more, over an appropriate period of time.*

The Work Team's task will be to consider, through group discussion and problem-solving, whether this Key Element is currently an agency strength, and if not, what might be needed, such as a new policy, training, or resource, to make it so.

Completion of all 25 components of the self-assessment will provide a thorough review of your agency's capacity to provide family reunification services, and a set of specific recommendations for improving your agency's policies, programs, training, and resources.

Staffing

Implementation of the Family Reunification Project requires the formation of three teams: an Implementation Team, a Management Team, and a Work Team. Their suggested composition, responsibilities, and expected time commitments are set forth below.

The Implementation Team

- Who: Top managers responsible for policy, program, training, and finance.

- Project Responsibility: Respond to the Family Reunification Project recommendations by planning and implementing system change.

13

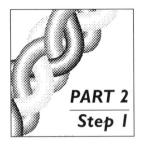

- Time Commitment: (1) half day—Orientation Meeting; (2) three, two-hour planning meetings with Management Team; and (3) full day—Planning for Change Meeting.

The Management Team

- Who: (1) Project Director—central office planner/administrator; and (2) Project Coordinator—staff supervisor.

- Project Responsibility: Plan and carry out Family Reunification Project activities, including launching the Family Reunification Project, conducting the assessment, and planning for system change.

- Time Commitment: (1) half day—Orientation Meeting; (2) five full days—conducting the assessment; (3) three, two-hour planning meetings with Implementation Team; (4) five, two-hour Management Team planning meetings; and (5) full day—Planning for Change Meeting.

The Work Team

- Who: The full range of staff involved with family reunification services, including administrators, supervisors, line staff, trainers, attorneys, parent aides, finance staff, foster parents, staff from community agencies, and biological parents. The Work Team should comprise about 15 people.

- Project Responsibility: Assess the agency's family reunification services and generate recommendations for improvement.

- Time Commitment: (1) half day—Orientation Meeting; (2) five full days—conducting the assessment; and (3) full day—Planning for Change Meeting.

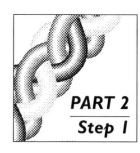

DECIDING TO UNDERTAKE THE PROJECT

The Challenge of Family Reunification

Why should your agency undertake a project with the scope of this one and the commitment it will demand of you? The reasons are as plentiful as the challenges that daily confront your agency. Child welfare agencies must be ready and able to:

- respond effectively to growing demands for family reunification services,

- seek out new opportunities to fund the development or expansion of family reunification services,

- manage changed staff/community expectations about children and families,

- comply with new mandates stemming from court decisions/legislatures,

- address critical evaluation results from external reviews, and

- handle problems that undermine family reunification services, such as inadequately trained staff, high foster parent turnover, and poor agency relationships with the legal system.

In addition to being an assessment instrument, the *Guide* is a teaching tool that will help you to respond to challenges like these. It contains the best thinking on the principles and strategies that promote sound family reunification policy and practice, and its comprehensive resources further inform participants about key aspects of family reunification service delivery. Thus, undertaking the Family Reunification Project exposes you and your staff to a wealth of family reunification theory, policy guidelines, and practice strategies, and helps you create action plans to respond to challenges such as those listed above.

Benefits of the Family Reunification Project

- The Family Reunification Project is a self-assessment tool, created by staff members who actually plan and implement family reunification services.

- The Family Reunification Project brings together the full range of players involved in family reunification work, to jointly consider current practices, identify problems, and work together to find solutions.

- The process of shared problem solving results in an empowered "we're in this together" attitude. Staff at all levels are reminded of how difficult it is to create and maintain a responsive child welfare system, and the part they themselves play in helping to shape the agency. There is less blame placed on the administration for problems, and more responsibility taken by each staff member for enhancing services.

- Participants get a tremendous morale and creativity boost and a renewed sense of optimism from having the opportunity to reflect on their work and

> Conducting the Family Reunification Project is an opportunity to convey our trust in staff. If we trust people enough to decide that a child will be safe if returned home, we should also trust them to come up with useful policy recommendations.
>
> —*Implementation Team Member*

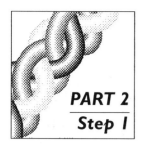

consider, through lively exchanges with coworkers, new and better ways to meet the needs of families and their children.

The model of self-assessment and planning for change featured here is a model that can be adapted to evaluate any function of your agency. The *Guide* can be used to examine and strengthen the full range of services your agency provides to children and their families.

Concerns about the Family Reunification Project

Obstacles to carrying out the Family Reunification Project will surely leap to any administrator's mind:

- Where will the time to carry out the Family Reunification Project come from?

- Where will the resources needed for system change come from?

These are valid questions. The words of an administrator who did decide to undertake the Family Reunification Project probably provide the best response:

We often feel that we don't have the resources to do it right the first time... but somehow we find the resources to do it wrong again and again.

Weighing the Benefits and Concerns

Use the space provided below to brainstorm with your administrative team about the benefits you can expect to derive from the Family Reunification Project, as well as the concerns you might have. Note ways of overcoming your concerns, then decide whether you are ready to undertake the Family Reunification Project.

Expected Benefits

_____
_____
_____
_____
_____

Concerns

_____
_____
_____
_____
_____

We can overcome our concerns by ...

_____
_____
_____
_____
_____

Decision

❏ Full steam ahead.   ❏ Proceed with caution and attention to concerns.

❏ Wait until a better time.

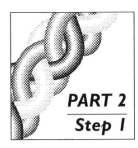
PUBLICIZING THE PROJECT

Once the decision has been made to undertake the Family Reunification Project, management's commitment to the process of self-assessment and system change should be conveyed to all staff as well as to relevant outside agencies. The Family Reunification Project provides an ideal opportunity to make known your agency's proactive stance toward improving the provision of services to children and families.

Publicity can take a variety of forms, including the following:

- Issue a communication to staff that announces the decision to undertake the Family Reunification Project, describes what the Family Reunification Project entails, and summarizes the expected outcomes and benefits to your agency.

- Issue a press release to inform other agencies and the community about the Family Reunification Project.

- Ask your agency's administrators to discuss the press release during a staff meeting.

- Include an announcement of the Family Reunification Project and its expected outcomes during relevant public presentations and meetings.

In the space below, or on a separate page, list ways in which you will publicize the Family Reunification Project.

We can publicize the Family Reunification Project by...

_____
_____
_____
_____
_____
_____
_____
_____
_____
_____
_____
_____
_____
_____
_____
_____
_____
_____
_____
_____

STEP TWO

FORMING THE TEAMS

Forming the
Implementation Team

Forming the
Management Team

Forming the
Work Team

RESPONSIBILITY

Senior-level managers

SUMMARY

Now that you have decided to undertake the Family Reunification Project, you are ready to form the three teams needed to plan and carry it out. STEP TWO describes the responsibilities of each team, lists the qualities and experiences each team member should have, and presents tips to ensure that you make sound team staffing choices.

FORMING THE IMPLEMENTATION TEAM

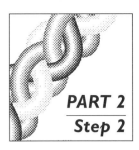

The Implementation Team comprises the top managers of your agency—those individuals responsible for such areas as policy, program, training, and finance. The Implementation Team should comprise about eight people.

Team Responsibilities

The Implementation Team's key function is to ensure that the Work Team's recommendations are carried out through changes in policy, program, training, and resource allocation. Other responsibilities include:

- sanctioning the project,
- outlining a planning process,
- choosing the management team,
- making available staff time and other resources, and
- participating in periodic progress and planning meetings.

Staffing

In selecting staff members to serve on the Implementation Team, look for those who:

- are committed to system change,
- understand and value the Family Reunification Project's goals and process,
- can draft policy and see it through to implementation,
- can direct modifications in program and training activities, and
- control—and can change—agency resource allocation.

In the space below, list those staff members whom you will ask to serve on the Implementation Team, as well as alternate choices.

Choices for Implementation Team	Alternate Choices
_____	_____
_____	_____
_____	_____
_____	_____
_____	_____
_____	_____
_____	_____

> It was a rare and rewarding opportunity to think about where we want the department to go...to get advice and insights from the staff who work with children and families every day...and to use their recommendations to plan and carry out needed improvements. It was great to be a part of such positive change.
>
> —*Implementation Team Member*

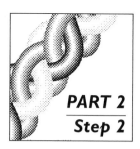
The Management Team comprises a Project Director and a Project Coordinator.

Selecting the Project Director

The Project Director is selected by the Implementation Team from those members of your central office staff who have planning/administration responsibilities.

Responsibilities

The Project Director takes charge of the Family Reunification Project by:

- participating in selecting the Project Coordinator and Work Team members;
- publicizing—inside and outside of the agency—the Family Reunification Project's mission and activities;
- planning and conducting the Orientation Meeting;
- participating in Work Team Meetings;
- serving on the Implementation Team, providing progress reports, and seeking consultation;
- planning and conducting the Planning for Change Meeting;
- informing and supporting system change activities; and
- consulting with the Project Coordinator.

Qualifications

In selecting a Project Director, look for a staff member who:

- is committed to system change,
- understands and values the Family Reunification Project's goals and process,
- has central office planning and administration responsibilities,
- is knowledgeable about agency policy and practices,
- has planned and carried out a time-limited project,
- supervises staff, and
- is respected by other staff.

In the space below, list the staff member whom you will ask to serve as Project Director, as well as an alternate choice.

> I have always been a behind-the-scenes person. Directing this Project has taught me that I have the skills to lead. I'm not good at just one thing. I can expand.
>
> —*Project Director*

Choice for Project Director   **Alternate Choice**

_____   _____

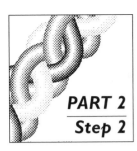

Selecting the Project Coordinator

The Project Coordinator should be selected by the Implementation Team and the Project Director from those members of your central office or regional staff who have supervisory responsibilities.

Responsibilities

The Project Coordinator facilitates the self-assessment process by:

- participating in selecting the Work Team members;
- planning and conducting the Orientation Meeting;
- chairing the Work Team Meetings;
- serving on the Implementation Team, providing progress reports, and seeking consultation;
- ensuring participation of outside experts;
- drafting and reviewing with the Work Team summaries of its meetings; and
- planning and conducting the Planning for Change Meeting.

Qualifications

In selecting a Project Coordinator, look for a staff member who:

- is committed to system change,
- understands and values the Family Reunification Project's goals and process,
- is able to lead and facilitate group discussion,
- is knowledgeable about agency policies and practices,
- is familiar with community resources and services,
- is well-organized,
- supervises staff, and
- is respected by other staff.

In the space below, list the staff member whom you will ask to serve as Project Coordinator, as well as an alternate choice.

Choice for Project Director   **Alternate Choice**

_____   _____

> The process was empowering. We had the opportunity to share our experiences, learn from each other, and collectively develop a vision of possibilities for our children and families.
>
> —Project Coordinator

TIPS FOR SUCCESS

- *Past Project Directors and Project Coordinators have been professionally enriched by heading the Family Reunification Project. It can be exciting to manage such an important effort toward improving family reunification services. When offering the positions, be sure to convey the importance of the undertaking and identify ways staff will benefit from the experience. (Participation should be voluntary.)*

- *Management Team members should be given reduced workloads or compensatory time in recognition of their participation.*

- *Once the Management Team is formed, the Project Director and Project Coordinator should each be given a copy of* Reconnecting Families: A Guide to Strengthening Family Reunification Services *to familiarize themselves completely with the Family Reunification Project and their responsibilities.*

FORMING THE WORK TEAM

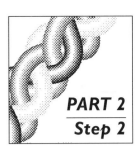
Members of the Work Team should be selected by the Implementation Team and Management Team from among those members of your central office staff who have responsibilities related to developing and/or delivering family reunification services. The Work Team should comprise about 15 people.

Responsibilities

Members of the Work Team carry out the self-assessment process by:

- evaluating the agency's family reunification policies, programs, and practices;

- generating a set of recommendations for improved service delivery; and

- collaborating with the Implementation Team on creating action plans for carrying out system change.

Qualifications

In selecting Work Team members, look for those who:

- are committed to system change,

- understand and value the Family Reunification Project's goals and process,

- are open to learning,

- are knowledgeable about family reunification service delivery, and

- represent the full range of players who are needed to plan and carry out reunification services. Consider including representatives of the following groups:

   —administrators

   —supervisors

   —line staff

   —trainers

   —finance staff

   —agency attorney

   —foster parents

   —biological parents

   —school personnel

   —staff from community provider agencies (e.g., drug and alcohol treatment services, schools, and specialized family reunification programs).

> I am grateful for the opportunity to discuss and share ideas for bringing about more effective ways to serve our children and families. The process was enlightening for the whole team.
>
> —*A Work Team Member*

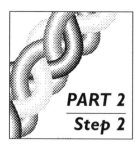

In the space provided below, list those staff members whom you will ask to serve on the Work Team, as well as alternate choices.

Choices for Work Team

_____
_____
_____
_____
_____
_____
_____
_____
_____
_____
_____
_____
_____
_____
_____
_____
_____

Alternate Choices for Work Team

_____
_____
_____
_____
_____
_____
_____
_____
_____
_____

TIPS FOR SUCCESS

- *If at all possible, participation on the Work Team should be voluntary. Work Team members should be given reduced workloads or compensatory time in recognition of their work on the Family Reunification Project.*

- *At the outset, you must decide whether you will (1) conduct the assessment in one region and then generalize the findings to the whole state, or (2) create a central Work Team with members from all regions.*

- *Since family reunification work is so closely involved with the judicial system, having an agency attorney as a member of the Work Team can be helpful.*

- *At least one Work Team member should be aware of central office policy and planning efforts. Ideally, this person will have a long history with the agency and will be privy to changes that may be coming.*

- *Be sure to convene a Work Team that culturally, racially, and ethnically reflects the composition of your agency and the population it serves.*

- *An intake social worker should be a member of the Work Team in order to reinforce the concept that placement is the first step toward reunification.*

STEP THREE

LAUNCHING THE PROJECT

Planning the Orientation Meeting

Conducting the Orientation Meeting

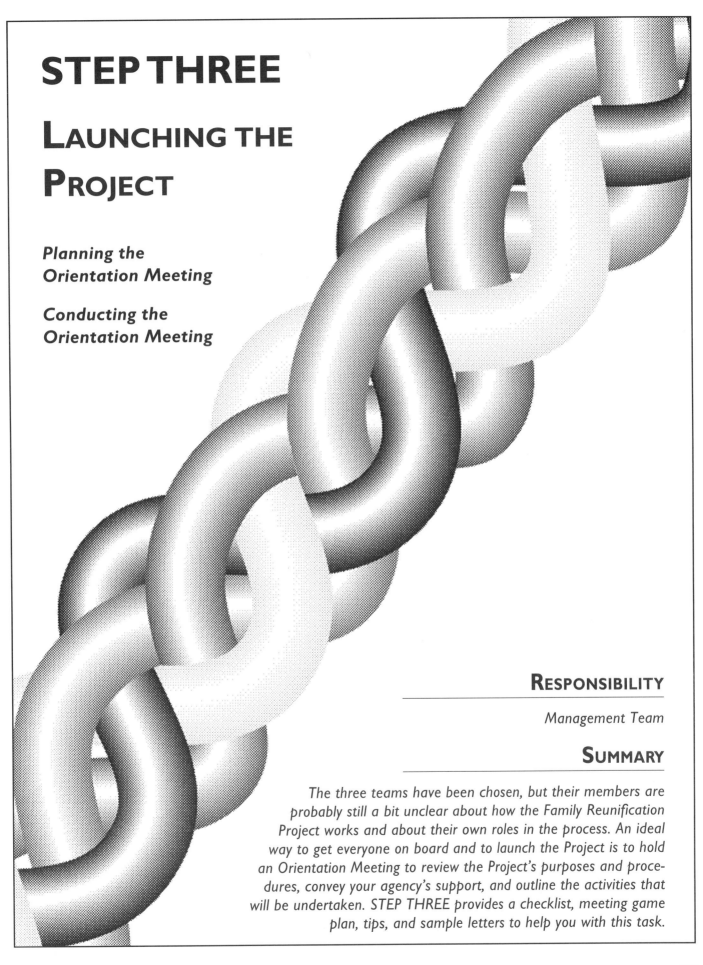

RESPONSIBILITY

Management Team

SUMMARY

The three teams have been chosen, but their members are probably still a bit unclear about how the Family Reunification Project works and about their own roles in the process. An ideal way to get everyone on board and to launch the Project is to hold an Orientation Meeting to review the Project's purposes and procedures, convey your agency's support, and outline the activities that will be undertaken. STEP THREE provides a checklist, meeting game plan, tips, and sample letters to help you with this task.

PLANNING THE ORIENTATION MEETING

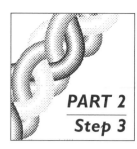

Selecting a Meeting Site and Time

Find a location outside of the agency to hold the Orientation Meeting. Plan on having lunch served. (Also identify a location away from the agency at which the Work Team meetings will be conducted.)

- The Orientation Meting will require three hours. Scheduling the Orientation Meeting from 10:00 A.M.—1:00 P.M. works well as the meeting can then include lunch.

Inviting Team Members

- Invite all Work Team and Implementation Team members to the Orientation Meeting. The Management Team should chair the Orientation Meeting.

  (A sample Orientation Meeting Invitation is provided on page 33.)

Establishing an Agenda

In preparation for the Orientation Meeting, create an agenda that reflects your purposes in holding the meeting. These purposes include the following:

- Explain the Family Reunification Project's objectives and expected outcomes.
- Convey your agency's support of the Family Reunification Project.
- Introduce members of the teams to each other and describe each team's responsibilities.
- Outline the activities that will be undertaken.

  (A sample Orientation Meeting Agenda is provided on page 34.)

TIPS FOR SUCCESS

- *If at all possible, your agency's Commissioner or Director should attend the Orientation Meeting, to signal interest and support at the highest level.*

- *It is important to hold the Family Reunification Project meetings out of the office and to serve food. The setting and food do not have to be fancy: the board room of a community agency and sandwiches or pizza go a long way toward letting people know they are appreciated.*

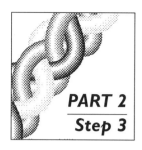

PART 2

Step 3

Scheduling Future Meetings

Develop a schedule of meeting dates, the components to be discussed at each, and a list of reading assignments.

(A sample Family Reunification Project Activity Schedule is provided on pages 35–36.)

Assembling Needed Materials

To conduct the Orientation Meeting, you will need to have your copy of *Reconnecting Families: A Guide to Strengthening Family Reunification Services*. In addition, each meeting participant will need a copy of the *Reconnecting Families Resource Workbook* (either a bound copy or one reproduced following the directions in the Appendix of the *Guide*) and a copy of *Together Again: Family Reunification in Foster Care*. Also, be sure to have on hand a flip chart and set of marking pens.

- Directions for assembling and photocopying the *Reconnecting Families Resource Workbook* may be found in the Appendix to the *Guide*. Bound copies of the *Resource Workbook* may be purchased from the Child Welfare League of America, using the form at the end of the *Guide*.

- *Together Again: Family Reunification in Foster Care*, edited by Barbara A. Pine, Robin Warsh, and Anthony N. Maluccio, and published by the Child Welfare League of America (1993), contains 11 chapters that members of the Work Team will need to read to prepare themselves to take part in the assessment. The book may be ordered from Child Welfare League of America, c/o CSSC, P.O. Box 7816, 300 Raritan Center Parkway, Edison, NJ 08818 (telephone 800/407–6273). Request stock #5251. A form for ordering the book may be found at the end of the *Guide*.

TIP FOR SUCCESS

- *Work Team Meetings should be held at least two weeks, though no more than one month, apart in order to allow time for members to attend to their professional responsibilities, as well as to read required material and reflect on the self-assessment process.*

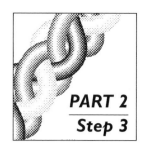
CONDUCTING THE ORIENTATION MEETING

Develop a plan for conducting the Orientation Meeting. The sample Game Plan provided below can guide you in carrying out a successful meeting.

Game Plan for Orientation Meeting—Agenda

- Welcome and Introductions—Management Team
- Overview of the Family Reunification Project—Project Director
- The Importance of System Change—Implementation Team
- Schedule of Activities—Project Coordinator
- Lunch
- Adjournment—Management Team

Welcome and Introductions (1 hour)

A useful opening exercise is to ask participants to state their name, title, and to complete this sentence: "One of the biggest obstacles families face on their path to reunification is..." Note their responses on a flip chart. This helps members to begin to consider their practice with children and families, and paints a picture of the many obstacles clients face, including:

- lack of community resources,
- lack of transportation and planning for family visits,
- tensions between biological and foster families,
- lack of specialized training and skill development for social workers,
- substance abuse,
- homelessness,
- difficulties with the court system,
- racism, and
- lack of aftercare services.

Overview of the Family Reunification Project (30 minutes)

1. Explain the purposes of the Family Reunification Project:
   - to identify the strengths and weaknesses of your agency's family reunification service delivery system, and
   - to develop an action plan for system change.

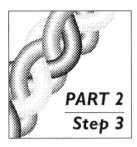

2. Establish the link between the obstacles listed on the flip chart and the components that will be examined during the self-assessment (e.g., Community Provider Agencies; Visiting; Foster Parent Roles and Responsibilities; Staff Development; Court and Legal Systems; Cultural Competence; and Postreunification Services.)

3. Distribute a copy of the *Reconnecting Families Resource Workbook* to each participant and describe its purposes and sections. Draw on the material included in the *Guide*'s introduction to organize your thoughts. Review and describe the contents of the Framework for Assessment of Strengths and Needs; the Key Elements for Success, and the worksheets participants will use in carrying out the actual assessments. (All of these may also be found in Part 3 of the *Guide*.) Step Four of Part 2, which begins on page 37 of the *Guide*, leads you through conducting the assessment.

4. Distribute a copy of *Together Again: Family Reunification in Foster Care* to each participant and explain that chapters will be assigned to be read in advance of each meeting. The readings will provide participants with the information they need to conduct the assessment effectively.

The Importance of System Change (15 minutes)

1. Convey the importance to your agency of the Family Reunification Project, the reasons it is being undertaken, and your commitment to addressing the recommendations that result from the assessment. It might be helpful to reread the benefits of and concerns about the Family Reunification Project that you listed on page 16 of the *Guide*.

2. Thank the Management Team and Work Team members for their willingness to participate in the Family Reunification Project.

Schedule of Activities (15 minutes)

Distribute an Activity Schedule for the Work Team, noting the topics to be covered, meeting dates, reading assignments, and meeting locations. Point out to Work Team members the chapters from *Together Again* that should be read for the first meeting (Chapters 1, 7, 8).

(A sample Family Reunification Project Activity Schedule is provided on pages 35–36.)

Adjournment (1 hour)

Following lunch, adjourn the Orientation Meeting by thanking everyone for their participation. Be sure to convey your sense of excitement and optimism that a process is beginning that will result in many needed changes.

ORIENTATION MEETING INVITATION

SAMPLE

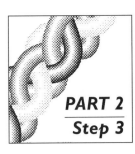

TO: Members of the Family Reunification Project

FROM: _____, Project Director

             _____, Project Coordinator

Thank you for agreeing to participate in the Family Reunification Project. The Project will help us to conduct a self-assessment of the strengths and weaknesses of our agency's family reunification service delivery system and develop an action plan for system change.

An Orientation Meeting will be held on March 15, 1995 from 10:00 A.M. to 1:00 P.M. at the Child and Family Services Board Room (see attached directions). At the meeting, we will explain further the Family Reunification Project's objectives and outline the activities we will undertake together.

As a member of the Family Reunification Project Work Team, you will be involved in five all-day sessions in which we will use the *Reconnecting Families Resource Workbook* and *Together Again: Family Reunification in Foster Care* to discuss our current family reunification policies and practices. Together, we will create a set of recommendations for improving service delivery to children and families separated by placement. The *Resource Workbook, Together Again,* and other materials will be given to you at the Orientation Meeting.

After we conclude the self-assessment, you will be involved in a day-long meeting to present our recommendations to our agency's administration, and to begin to create an action plan for system change.

We look forward to meeting with you next month. Should you have any questions, please feel free to contact _____ at _____.

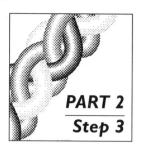

**Family Reunification Project
Orientation Meeting Agenda**

March 15, 1995 • 10:00 A.M.–1:00 P.M.
Child and Family Services Board Room

Purpose

- To explain the objectives of the Family Reunification Project and outline the activities to be undertaken

Schedule

- Welcome and Introductions—Management Team
- Overview of the Family Reunification Project—Project Director
- The Importance of System Change—Implementation Team
- Schedule of Activities—Project Coordinator
- Lunch
- Adjournment—Management Team

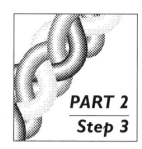
Meeting I—April 19 (9:30 A.M.–3:30 P.M.)

Component	**Read from Together Again**
• Mission and Principles	• Chapter 1: "Family Reunification: An Overview"
• Preparing Children for Reunification	• Chapter 7: "Visiting: The Heart of Reunification"
• Visiting	• Chapter 8: "Preparing Children for Reunification"

Meeting II—May 20 (9:30 A.M.–3:30 P.M.)

Component	**Read from Together Again**
• Preparing Families for Reunification	• Chapter 9: "Believing in Families"
• Foster Parent Roles and Responsibilities	
• Social Worker Roles and Responsibilities	
• Recruitment	

Meeting III—June 18 (9:30 A.M.–3:30 P.M.)

Component	**Read from Together Again**
• Cultural Competence	• Chapter 5: "Goal Setting with Biological Families"
• Assessment and Goal Planning	• Chapter 10: "Evaluating Family Reunification Programs"
• Program Monitoring and Evaluation	• Chapter 11: "The Interaction of Research and Practice in Family Reunification"
• Workloads	
• The Work Environment	
• Funding Sources	

Meeting IV—June 21 (9:30 A.M.–3:30 P.M.)

Component	**Read from Together Again**
• Staff Development	• Chapter 2: "Building Court-Agency Partnerships to Reunify Families"
• Supervision	• Chapter 3: "Training for Competence in Family Reunification Practice"
• School Systems	
• Court and Legal Systems	
• Law Enforcement Agencies	
• External Reviewers	

continued…

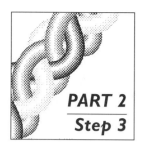

Meeting V—August 18 (9:30 A.M.–3:30 P.M.)*

Component

- Financial Management
- Public Relations and Information
- Community Provider Agencies
- Postreunification Services
- Governmental Bodies
- Cross-System Collaboration

Read from Together Again

- Chapter 4: "Family Reunification Practice in a Community-Based Mental Health Center"
- Chapter 6: "Family Reunification Practice in Residential Treatment for Children"

*Note: Time will also be allotted to design the Planning for Change Meeting.

Planning for Change Meeting— September 30 (9:30 A.M.–3:30 P.M.)

1. Present recommendations to the agency administration and begin to create an action plan for change.

Please note...

All *Work Team Meetings* will be held in the Board Room of Child and Family Services. The *Planning for Change Meeting* will be held at the Woodlawn Retreat.

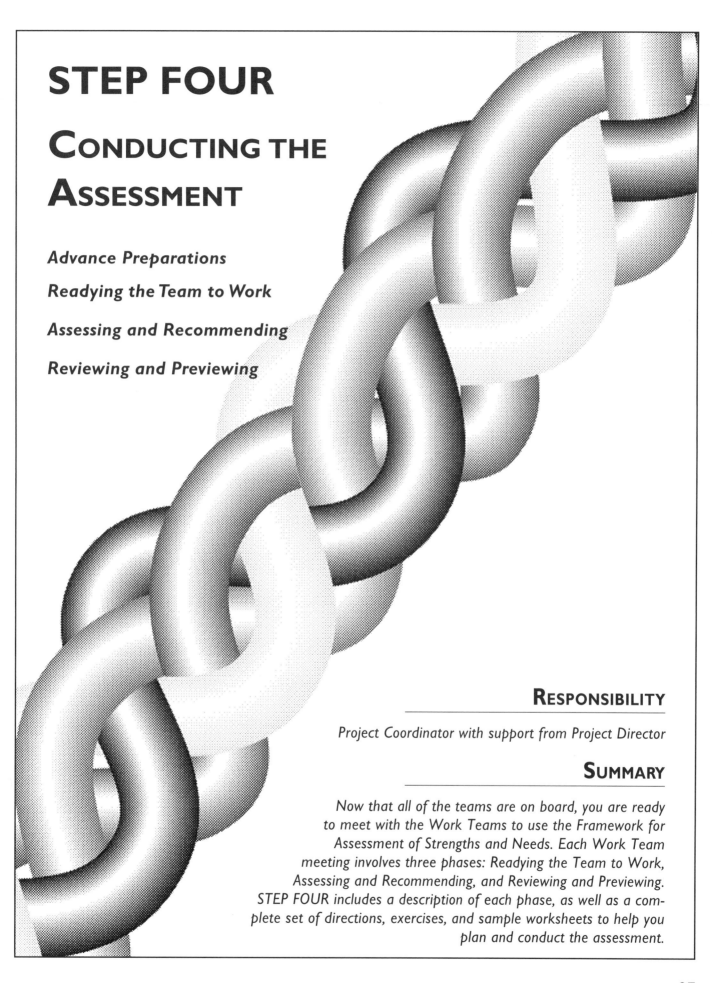

STEP FOUR

CONDUCTING THE ASSESSMENT

Advance Preparations

Readying the Team to Work

Assessing and Recommending

Reviewing and Previewing

SUMMARY

Now that all of the teams are on board, you are ready to meet with the Work Teams to use the Framework for Assessment of Strengths and Needs. Each Work Team meeting involves three phases: Readying the Team to Work, Assessing and Recommending, and Reviewing and Previewing. STEP FOUR includes a description of each phase, as well as a complete set of directions, exercises, and sample worksheets to help you plan and conduct the assessment.

37

ADVANCE PREPARATIONS

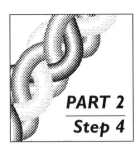

Before the first of the five all-day Work Team Meetings...

1. If you have not already done so, secure a location outside of the agency's offices to hold the Work Team Meetings (e.g., the board room of a community agency or public library).

   - Arrange for lunch to be served.

   - Be sure the room is equipped with an easel, flip chart, and markers.

2. Identify and invite outside experts to take part in selected meetings (e.g., invite police to take part in the meeting concerning Law Enforcement Agencies, and biological parents to the meeting concerning Preparing Families for Reunification).

   - Consider inviting central office managers, especially when evaluating the following components: recruitment, funding sources, governmental bodies, and external reviewers.

3. Invite members of the Implementation Team to attend any or all Work Team Meetings.

4. Have on hand additional copies of the *Reconnecting Families Resource Workbook, Together Again: Reconnecting Families in Foster Care*, notepaper, and pens.

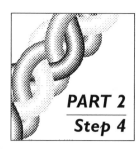
At the start of each Work Team Meeting, the Project Coordinator, with support from the Project Director, should

- introduce any outside experts,

- conduct an opening exercise,

- highlight the Components to be covered that day, and

- obtain approval from the Work Team of the summary of recommendations from the previous session.

Introducing Outside Experts

Introduce any outside experts such as law enforcement and school personnel. Review briefly the Family Reunification Project purposes and expected outcomes.

Conducting an Opening Exercise

Conduct an opening exercise to get everyone thinking about family reunification service delivery. Several examples of opening exercises are provided below.

Word Association

Purpose: To help Work Team members identify their own biases, stereotypes, and expectations in relation to being part of the Family Reunification Project.

  Directions: Ask Work Team members to write down the first word(s) that comes to mind when you say the following:

- (name of your agency)
- System change
- Foster parents

- Biological family
- Family reunification

  Ask Work Team members to use their responses to consider the strengths they bring to the Family Reunification Project. Invite volunteers to share their strengths.

TIPS FOR SUCCESS

- *Outside experts will not be needed for the first meeting. Not having outsiders present gives the Work Team an opportunity to begin to coalesce.*

- *Once you start to meet with members of the Work Team, be sure to solicit their suggestions for the names of outside experts to invite to future meetings.*

- *Whenever outside experts participate in a Work Team meeting, allow additional time for discussion: it will be needed as this "new" team forms and establishes a way to work together.*

41

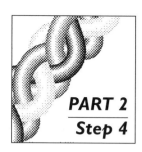

PART 2

Step 4

Success Stories (to be used after the second meeting)

Purpose: To identify and share ways in which the Family Reunification Project is enhancing Work Team members' practice with children and families.

Directions: Ask the Work Team members to take a few moments to consider whether they have a success story to share—an example of how their work has been positively shaped by their participation in the Family Reunification Project.

Highest Priority

Purpose: To reinforce the Family Reunification Project's focus on system change.

Directions: Ask Work Team members to write down the one change, in policy, training, or resource allocation, that they most want the agency to implement as a result of undertaking the Family Reunification Project. Those who are willing can share their response.

Midpoint Check (to be used at the beginning of the third or fourth meeting)

Purpose: To determine if the process for conducting the assessment can be improved in any way.

Directions: Recap briefly the process that has been used to assess the Components. Facilitate discussion of modifications that may be needed.

Highlighting the Components

Highlight the Component to be covered that day (e.g., Mission and Principles, Preparing Children for Reunification, Visiting).

Approving the Summary of Recommendations

The Project Coordinator should prepare a "Summary of Work Team Recommendations" following each meeting (see the information on Reviewing and Previewing on page 45). The Work Team should approve this summary before beginning its work on the next Component set.

(A sample Summary of Work Team Recommendations is provided on page 49.)

TIP FOR SUCCESS

• *A good way to move into the review of the "Summary of Work Team Recommendations" from the prior meeting is to recap the Components that were assessed and ask, "How has your work been influenced by our discussion of... (e.g., Preparing Families for Reunification)?"*

ASSESSING AND RECOMMENDING

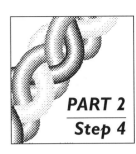

After completion of the opening exercises, introductions, and approval of the recommendations from the prior session, the Work Team members should collectively:

- discuss their reactions to the readings,
- review each Component's Key Elements for Success,
- share ideas about your agency strengths and needs in relation to the Key Elements for Success,
- make policy, training, and resource allocation recommendations to improve your agency's family reunification delivery system.

Reacting to the Readings

To promote a free-flowing discussion by Work Team members, use open-ended questions such as:

- What were your reactions when you read _____?
- What is one idea presented in _____ that really made an impression on you?

Reviewing Each Component's Key Elements for Success

1. Read the entire list of elements aloud.

2. Have the Work Team members use the "Strengths and Needs Worksheet" for each Component to write down their ideas about what they see as agency strengths and needs in relation to the Key Elements for Success.

   (A sample of how one Work Team member completed a Strengths and Needs Worksheet is provided on page 47.)

3. Lead the Work Team in a discussion of the strengths and needs they have identified. Some useful ways to do that are:

   - Ask Work Team members, "How well do you think our agency is doing in relation to these Key Elements for _____?"
   - Ask Work Team members, "As you look at the list, what do we do well, and what do we need to do better?"

TIP FOR SUCCESS

- *Be prepared to open up with your own reactions to the readings if the Work Team members are having a hard time getting started.*

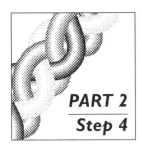

- Have Work Team members complete the sentence, "I'd be a more effective social worker if…" (or "I'd be more effective at family visiting…assessment and goal planning…delivering postreunification services…").

4. Encourage discussion that results in identifying the needs that Work Team members must have met in order to do their work effectively as set forth in the Key Elements.

Recommending Improvements in Service Delivery

1. Build on the previous discussion of strengths and needs to help the Work Team members formulate specific policy, training, and resource recommendations that the agency should act on to bring about system change. Have members write their ideas on the "Assessment and Recommendation Worksheets."

   (A sample of how one Work Team member completed an Assessment and Recommendation Worksheet is provided on page 48.)

2. Lead the Work Team members in a discussion of their recommendations. Some helpful ways to do that are:

   - Ask "What should be conveyed to the Implementation Team about the changes we need to make?"

   - Tell Work Team members, "This is a magic wand group. If you could wave a wand and improve our practice in the area of _____, what would you do?"

3. Encourage discussion that leads to clarification and consensus on recommendations being made.

4. Use a large flip chart and easel to note recommendations. Place a "P" after those requiring a new policy; a "T" after those involving training; and an "R" after those requiring a change in resources. This will make the task of drafting the "Summary of Work Team Recommendations" easier (see page 45).

TIPS FOR SUCCESS

- *Encourage members to offer examples from their practice to support their assessment of the Key Elements.*

- *As members begin to compare their lists with the reality of agency life, they may feel frustrated, overwhelmed, and doubtful that needed improvements will be made. Should such feelings occur, it is important that they be acknowledged, and that the Work Team be reminded that your agency, by supporting the Family Reunification Project, is committed to change through this process of assessment, recommendation, and implementation.*

- *Trust the process! At times, especially during the first and second meetings, Work Team members may have difficulty confining their comments to the Component being discussed. An accurate assessment of strengths and needs requires a compartmentalized look at family reunification. In time, Work Team members will grow accustomed to focusing on one Component at a time. To bring the Work Team back on track, say "We seem to have gotten away from the (total number) Key Elements listed here. Maybe we could take a look at each of the Key Elements one by one and talk about what we think our agency's strengths and weaknesses are and why."*

- *Enlist the help of a Work Team member to write on the flip chart so that you can concentrate on helping the group clarify its thinking about its recommendations.*

- *Take the opportunity to point out how complex it is to make sound recommendations and to empathize with administrators about the difficult job they have in creating a responsive child welfare system.*

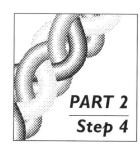

In this phase, the Project Director and Project Coordinator:

- summarize the Work Team recommendations,

- acknowledge the good job the Work Team has done,

- identify the Components to be addressed at the next meeting, and the suggested reading assignments, and

- categorize the Work Team recommendations.

Summarizing/Acknowledgments

The Project Director and Project Coordinator should help the Work Team members to see how much they have accomplished during their time together, and keep them motivated to continue working. One way to do that is to say something like:

> "This has been a very valuable day and I thank you. We've generated over 30 ideas for improving our reunification services. I'll have a summary of our Work Team Recommendations typed for you to review at our next meeting. What stands out to me most from today's assessment is our need to collaborate better with outside agencies, and to learn new ways to involve families in the reunification effort."

A form for summarizing the Work Team Recommendations may be found in and reproduced from Part 7 of the *Guide*, or you may create your own.

(A sample Summary of Work Team Recommendations is provided on page 49.)

Identifying Components for the Next Meeting

Direct the Work Team's attention to the topics for next time. Review the assigned readings and briefly describe why they are important (e.g., the reading on visiting contains a sample visit report form that the Work Team members might find useful). Decide who should be invited to serve as outside experts at the next meeting.

TIP FOR SUCCESS

- *One way to expand the number of staff who are involved in the assessment process is to ask the Work Team members to poll their colleagues on their concerns and issues in relation to the Components that will be addressed next time. This helps to make additional staff aware of the Project and will enhance the assessment.*

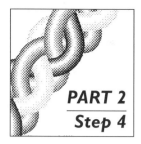

Categorizing the Recommendations/Next Steps

1. Set aside part of the afternoon of the last Work Team Meeting to discuss the purposes of, and establish an agenda for, the Planning for Change Meeting (see pages 51–63).

2. Following the last meeting of the Work Team, you will need to organize a final "Report of the Work Team: Recommendations for Strengthening our Family Reunification Services" for use by all three teams, and others, in planning for system change. Forms for the Report of the Work Team may be found in and reproduced from Part 7 of the *Guide*, or you may create your own.

   (A sample from a Report of the Work Team is provided on page 50.)

3. In preparing for the Planning for Change Meeting, distribute a copy of the "Report of the Work Team" at least one week prior to the meeting to all those invited. Ask them to bring their copy with them.

TIPS FOR SUCCESS

- *A good way to categorize the recommendations is according to the nine principles of family reunification that were discussed during the Work Team's first meeting. This gives the Work Team members an opportunity to place their recommendations within the context of a philosophical approach to reunification.*

The Principles

A. *With its emphasis on ensuring continuity of relationships and care for children, family reunification is an integral part of the philosophy of permanency planning.*

B. *Children are best reared in families, preferably their own; most families can care for their own children if properly assisted.*

C. *Family reunification practice must be guided by an ecologically oriented, competence-centered perspective, that emphasizes:*

   - *promoting family empowerment,*

   - *engaging in advocacy and social action,*

   - *reaching for—and building on—family strengths,*

   - *involving any and all whom the child considers family as partners, and*

   - *providing needed services and supports.*

D. *Teamwork among the many parties involved in family reunification is critical.*

E. *All forms of human diversity—ethnic, racial, cultural, religious, life-style—as well as physical and mental challenges, must be respected.*

F. *A commitment to early and consistent child-family visiting is an essential ingredient in preparing for—and maintaining—reunification.*

G. *Foster parents and child care workers must be involved as members of the service delivery team. The agency should share information with them about the child and family that is shared with other service providers, involve them in decisions, and provide them with adequate training.*

H. *Many families will have continuing service needs in multiple areas. Services to meet these needs must be provided for as long as children and families require them to maintain the reunification.*

I. *Agencies must empower their staffs by providing adequate training and supervision and by using a team approach in making case decisions.*

---

7. SOCIAL WORKER ROLES AND RESPONSIBILITIES

Strengths and Needs Worksheet
SAMPLE

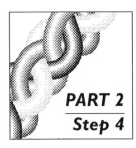

Directions

Review the key elements for *Component #7: Social Worker Roles and Responsibilities*, and any other related material. Consider what supports or hinders social workers in carrying out their work to reunify families. Note these supports (strengths) and hindrances (needs) below in preparation for the Work Team discussion. Use additional pages if necessary.

Strengths

1. We tell parents, right at the time of placement, that we're going to work with them to help them get their kids back home.

2. We do everything we can to have parents visit with their kids as soon as possible after placement, and, unless there's a reason not to, the visits take place every week.

Needs

1. We need more training on helping parents evaluate their ability to parent, and on helping them correct the problems that led to placement.

2. We don't know how to help kids and parents to make a placement diary, or how to use it with them to help with reunification.

47

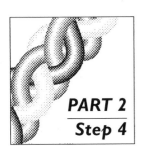

Specific Policy Recommendations

We need to require written visiting plans that specify visit purposes; frequency; length; location; supervision; participants; any supportive services; and planned activities.

Specific Training Recommendations

Staff needs to learn more about how to help children, parents, and foster parents prepare for and work through their reactions to visits.

Specific Resource Recommendations

There need to be more vehicles for transportation. They should be large (station wagons or vans), air-conditioned, equipped with safety locks and windows, and able to accommodate car seats.

Date: ___/___/____   Work Team: _____

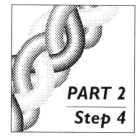

Component #: *12 Assessment and Goal Planning*

Policy Recommendations

1. Treatment plans need to be written first and foremost for the clients, using their language.

2. The Department needs to ensure that collaborating agencies work to support one agreed-upon service plan.

3. At least one administrative case review needs to take place in the family's home.

4. A multiagency goal-planning orientation needs to be promoted so that there is only one service plan per family.

Training Recommendations

1. Staff members need to know how to assess the impact on the child and family of experiences that led to the need for placement, the family's communication patterns, and the family's conflict resolution skills.

2. Staff members need to learn how to develop service plans that are strength focused and capacity building.

Resource Recommendations

1. A meeting space large enough for all those involved in the reunification effort to convene needs to be found.

2. A service plan that all providers can use needs to be developed.

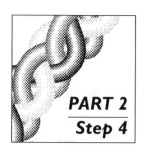

REPORT OF THE WORK TEAM

Principle A

With its emphasis on ensuring continuity of relationships and care for children, family reunification is an integral part of the philosophy of permanency planning.

In order to accomplish this, we recommend that:

1. The Department's commitment to reunification needs to be conveyed to all parties involved in the reunification effort by social workers as soon as the decision to place is made.

2. There needs to be a policy statement that addresses the importance of continuity of workers to children and families. There needs to be a limit established on the number of times a case can be transferred.

STEP FIVE

PLANNING FOR CHANGE

Advance Preparations

Conducting the Planning for Change Meeting

Bringing Closure to the Project

RESPONSIBILITY

Management Team

SUMMARY

Completing the Family Reunification Project involves bringing the three teams together to establish a plan for creating system change. One way to do this is to hold a day-long meeting to examine the results of the assessment and jointly consider strategies for implementing policy, program, resource, and training changes. STEP FIVE provides the guidance needed to plan and carry out this meeting, as well as to bring closure to the Family Reunification Project.

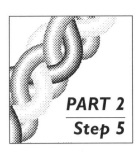
Selecting a Meeting Site and Time

As was done for the Orientation and Work Team Meetings, find a location outside of the agency to hold the Planning for Change Meeting. Plan on having lunch served. If the meeting will start early in the morning, arrange to have coffee and other appropriate refreshments.

Inviting All Participants

Invite all those who participated in the Family Reunification Project to the Planning for Change Meeting. Extend the invitation to other key personnel, such as deputy commissioners, regional directors, planners, and public information staff.

(A sample Planning for Change Meeting Invitation is provided on page 58.)

Establishing an Agenda

Set aside the afternoon of the last Work Team Meeting to discuss the purposes of and establish an agenda for the Planning for Change Meeting. The purposes of the Planning for Change Meeting include the following:

- Recognize the commitment and hard work of the three teams.
- Reinforce administrative commitment to making needed changes.
- Share the "flavor" of the assessment process.
- Review the content of the recommendations.
- Convey what the Work Team has learned about family reunification from having taken part in the Family Reunification Project,
- Apply a model for planning system change that can be ongoing in the agency.
- Begin to develop a plan to implement the recommendations.

(A sample Planning for Change Meeting Agenda is provided on page 59.)

TIPS FOR SUCCESS

- *Remember the importance of creature comforts. People appreciate adequate meeting space, an attractive setting, large windows and good food. If at all possible, don't skimp on these. Large corporations will often contribute meeting space to nonprofit agencies. Ask around.*

- *The agency might benefit by expanding the invitation to include media representatives, legislators, federal officers, staff from private child advocacy agencies, and administrators of related departments, such as mental health or juvenile justice.*

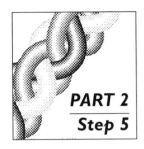

Assembling Materials

Make copies of all materials needed for participants' meeting packets. Use colorful folders to hold the materials, indicating on the cover the name of the meeting, your agency's name, and the date. The packet should include copies of the following materials:

- Planning for Change Meeting Agenda

- Family Reunification: An Expanded Definition

- The Principles of Family Reunification

- The Components of Family Reunification

- Sample of Key Elements—Visiting

- Action Planning for Family Reunification (directions for small-group activity) and Action Plan form.

- Planning for Change Meeting Evaluation

  (Samples of the Planning for Change Meeting Agenda, Action Planning for Family Reunification (directions) and Action Plan form, and Planning for Change Meeting Evaluation may be found on pages 59–63. Copies for reproduction of Family Reunification: An Expanded Definition, The Principles of Family Reunification, The Components of Family Reunification, Sample of Key Elements—Visiting, Action Planning for Family Reunification (directions) and Action Plan form, and Planning for Change Meeting Evaluation may be found in Part 7: Additional Forms of the Guide.)

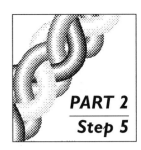

CONDUCTING THE
PLANNING FOR CHANGE MEETING

Develop a plan for conducting the Planning for Change Meeting. The sample game plan provided below can guide you in carrying out a successful meeting.

Game Plan for Planning for Change Meeting—Agenda

- Welcome and Introductions—Management Team
- Overview of the Project—Management Team
- The Agency Perspective—Agency Commissioner or Director
- A New Look at Family Reunification—Project Director or Project Coordinator
- Results of the Project: Recommendations for Change—Management Team
- Lunch
- Practice Session: Creating Plans for Change—Management Team
- Where Do We Go from Here?—Management Team
- Closing Ceremony—Agency Commissioner or Director

Welcome and Introductions (15 minutes)

The Management Team presents an overview of the day's schedule, makes necessary introductions, and conveys thanks to all involved.

Overview of the Project (15 minutes)

The Management Team describes briefly the assessment process, including the Components discussed, the method used for assessing the Key Elements, and the recommendations generated.

Refer participants to their packets, which contain the expanded definition of family reunification, the list of the 25 components, and a sample Key Element for Success.

(Copies of these materials suitable for reproduction may be found in Part 7 of the Guide.*)*

> "We began from different perspectives, agreed to commonalities, and moved forward together, in order to facilitate change for children and families who need assistance."
>
> —*Work Team Member*

> "The meetings heightened my awareness of the importance of children growing up in a family system. I've been working differently with families. . . It's really important that we do all that we can to help them get back together."
>
> —*Work Team Member*

TIP FOR SUCCESS

- *Solicit a quote from each of the Work Team members that captures what it meant for them to be involved in the Project. Write each quote, along with the person's name, on newsprint and display the quotes on the walls of the meeting room for all to read. The Management Team, or a Work Team member, might also read the quotes as part of the "Welcome and Introductions." The sharing of the quotes is a powerful and effective way to help the Implementation Team appreciate the experience of the Work Team and to recognize the importance of making needed changes.*

55

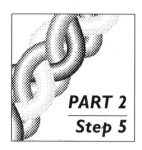

The Agency Perspective (15 minutes)

The Commissioner or Director talks briefly about the importance of the Family Reunification Project and the agency's commitment to change. This is an ideal time for top management to talk about the future directions for the agency and the importance of the Family Reunification Project in shaping those directions, and most importantly, to recognize the accomplishments and dedication of the various teams.

A New Look at Reunification (15 minutes)

The Project Director or Project Coordinator conveys some of the new family reunification concepts that were learned through taking part in the Family Reunification Project, and discusses the impact of these concepts on the self-assessment.

Results of the Project: Recommendations for Change (1 hour)

To review selected recommendations and begin the planning process, the Management Team asks the participants to join one of nine groups, each of which works on one of the nine principles that were discussed during the first meeting of the Work Team. Using the final "Report of the Work Team" and the "Action Plan" directions and form, each group reviews the list of recommendations associated with their principle and selects one to turn into an action plan for change.

> *(A sample Report of the Work Team may be found on page 50; a sample Action Plan may be found on pages 60–62. Copies suitable for reproduction may be found in Part 7 of the* Guide.*)*

Lunch (1 hour)

Practice Session: Creating Plans for Change (2 hours)

The Management Team asks the nine small groups to reconvene and to continue their work on their "Action Plans." They should work for about 90 minutes at devising a set of "Action Steps" to implement their recommendation.

> *(Samples of these materials are provided on pages 60–62. Copies suitable for reproduction may be found in Part 7 of the* Guide.*)*

During the final 30 minutes, each group provides a summary of their plans to the group as a whole.

Where Do We Go From Here? (15 minutes)

The Management Team reiterates that the process used for creating the nine action plans is an ideal one for addressing the remaining recommendations contained in the "Report of the Work Team."

TIP FOR SUCCESS

• *Participants can work at nine separate tables, each marked with the letter A through I, to correspond to each of the principles. Also, for ease of reference, and in case any participants forget to bring the reports with them, prepare a handout for each group, with each principle stated on top, followed by the corresponding recommendations.*

Bringing Closure to the Project

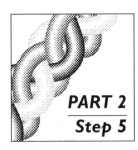

After months of meeting and working together, it is time to mark the close of the Family Reunification Project.

Wrapping Up

The Management Team offers some reflections on what it has been like to lead the Family Reunification Project, including what they have learned, and again thanks all participants.

- The Commissioner or Director responds to the day's events, reaffirms the agency's commitment to acting on the findings of the Work Team, and thanks everyone.

- The Management Team asks all participants to complete the evaluation form contained in their packets.

    (A sample Evaluation Form is provided on page 63. A copy suitable for reproduction may be found in Part 7 of the Guide.)

- The Commissioner or Director sends all participants a follow-up thank you letter.

Closing Ceremony

The Commissioner or Director presents each member of the Work Team with a certificate in recognition of their participation in the Family Reunification Project.

(A certificate suitable for reproduction and completion may be found in Part 7 of the Guide or your agency may devise its own.)

> There seemed to be a special closeness of people gathered for a common purpose—to create a better system to help families. It was refreshing to have my input valued. I believe real good will come from this effort.
>
> —*Implementation Team Member*

TIP FOR SUCCESS

- *In addition to being a work session, the meeting is a day of celebration and salute to dedicated staff and forward-looking management. Be creative in finding other ways to express appreciation and camaraderie, including t-shirts, coffee mugs, and a group photograph.*

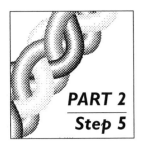

PLANNING FOR CHANGE MEETING INVITATION

SAMPLE

TO: Members of the Family Reunification Project

FROM: _____, Project Director

             _____, Project Coordinator

We are pleased to report that the assessment of our agency's family reunification service system conducted by the Work Team is complete; the Report of the Work Team will be forwarded to you shortly.

Please join us at a day-long meeting: "The Family Reunification Project: Planning for Change," on September 30, from 9:30 A.M. to 3:30 P.M., at the Woodlawn Retreat (see attached directions). At this Planning for Change Meeting, we will review the Work Team's recommendations and begin to create an action plan for system change.

We look forward to seeing you next month. Should you have any questions, or if you are unable to attend, please feel free to contact _____ at _____.

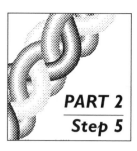
Family Reunification Project
Planning for Change Meeting Agenda

September 30, 1995 • 9:30 A.M.–3:30 P.M.
Woodlawn Retreat

Purpose

- To review the Family Reunification Project recommendations and begin to create an action plan for system change

Schedule

- Welcome and Introductions—Management Team

- Overview of the Project—Management Team

- The Agency Perspective—Agency Commissioner or Director

- A New Look at Family Reunification—Project Director or Project Coordinator

- Results of the Project: Recommendations for Change—Management Team

- Lunch

- Practice Session: Creating Plans for Change—Management Team

- Where Do We Go from Here?—Management Team

- Closing Ceremony—Agency Commissioner or Director

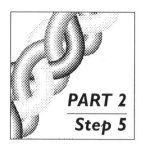

ACTION PLANNING FOR FAMILY REUNIFICATION

Directions for Small-Group Activity

This activity involves small groups of members of all of the Family Reunification Project teams, as well as invited guests, working together to turn the recommendations of the Work Team into a beginning set of action plans for the agency. The main purposes of the exercise are to:

- clarify the issues and concerns (and personal experiences) discussed in the Work Team meetings that led to the recommendation;

- provide an opportunity for agency staff members to consider how they might contribute to making the recommended change in the service delivery system, whether that contribution is at the policy level, administrative level, or practice level; and

- implement an action planning process that will result in a plan to address at least one recommendation in each small group.

The activity is conducted in two parts. Part I (one hour) focuses on each group's discussion of the recommendations under one of the principles that form the framework for the Work Team Final Report. By the conclusion of Part I, each group will select one recommendation to work on during the afternoon session, based on the following criteria:

- The agency could feasibly plan and accomplish some action steps to achieve the recommendation within the next six months to a year.

- The action plan for addressing the recommendation would make the most use of the potential contributions of the members of the small group.

- Implementing the recommendation would make a significant contribution to improving the agency's ability as an agency to reconnect families.

In Part II, the small groups develop and prepare to present an action plan (90 minutes). Each small group then reports out to the group as a whole (30 minutes).

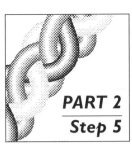

SAMPLE

Use this planning tool to turn each of the recommendations of the Work Team into a set of action plans for the agency.

Principle: D

Teamwork among the many parties involved in family reunification is critical.

_____

_____

_____

Work Team Recommendation

A forum needs to be convened between our agency and judicial staff to bring to the surface and address the many issues that create tensions between the systems and result in ineffective reunification service delivery.

Key Issues Related to This Recommendation

(i.e., What is the rationale for this recommendation? What examples from your practice support this needed change? What additional comments or questions do you have about it?)

The Department and the court system are often in conflict. For example, the attorney general's office doesn't keep us informed of statutory changes and appellate decisions that impact reunification practice; the Department and court personnel define "reasonable efforts" differently.

_____

_____

_____

_____

_____

_____

_____

_____

_____

_____

_____

_____

_____

61

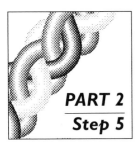
Action Steps Needed

1. Create forum planning committee, composed of agency and judicial staff.

2. Establish specific forum purposes and goals.

3. Identify forum participants and facilitator.

4. Send invitation letter from Commissioner and Administrative Judge.

5. At forum—identify what is working and what is not.

6. Develop plans to build on things that work and modify those that don't.

7. Identify needed changes in policy and procedures.

8. Develop implementation plans.

Resources and Supports Needed for Implementation

(i.e., what obstacles must be overcome, and what resources are needed to carry out the action steps successfully in such areas as space, personnel, time, money, and sanctions?)

Obstacles: lack of communication between the two systems may make it hard to even create the committee resource.

Needed: "buy-in" at top of both systems.

Measures of Success (in six months)

1. Planning committee created.

2. Forum purposes and goals established.

3. Forum fully planned.

4. Participants identified and invited.

Measures of Success (in one year)

1. Convened forum; identified needed changes.

2. Created implementation plan.

3. Created court-agency coalition to monitor progress of above plan and serve as "watchdog" for any problem areas that need to be addressed.

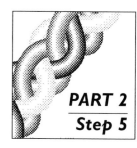

PLANNING FOR CHANGE MEETING EVALUATION

The overall purposes of this meeting are to examine the results of the self-assessment of our family reunification services and begin to create an action plan for system change.

To what extent did the following aspects of the meeting help or hinder achieving these purposes?

- the introductory sessions:

_____

_____

_____

- the small group exercise:

_____

_____

_____

- the mix of participants:

_____

_____

_____

- the written materials:

_____

_____

_____

- the facility:

_____

_____

_____

- other:

_____

_____

_____

STEP SIX

EVALUATING THE FAMILY REUNIFICATION PROJECT

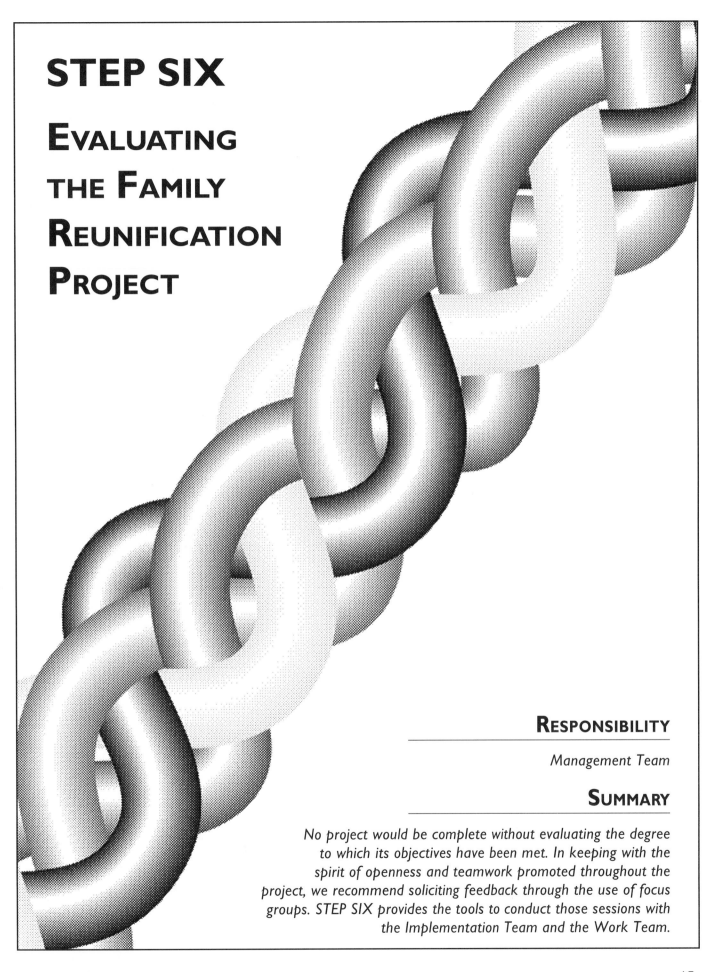

RESPONSIBILITY

Management Team

SUMMARY

No project would be complete without evaluating the degree to which its objectives have been met. In keeping with the spirit of openness and teamwork promoted throughout the project, we recommend soliciting feedback through the use of focus groups. STEP SIX provides the tools to conduct those sessions with the Implementation Team and the Work Team.

EVALUATING THE FAMILY REUNIFICATION PROJECT

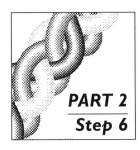
Purpose

Now that the Family Reunification Project is over, the Implementation and Work Team members should be given time to discuss their reactions to the work that has taken place, as well as their thoughts about the work that remains. The Management Team should:

- solicit feedback from and about the Implementation Team and the Work Team, and

- identify the potential for, and initial evidence of, change.

Procedure

Within one month of holding the Planning for Change Meeting, the Management Team should schedule 45-minutes Focus Group Sessions with the Implementation Team and the Work Team members to get their reactions to the Family Reunification Project and to the *Guide*. Each team should have its own session. The sessions can be taped or notes can be taken for future reference.

Focus Group Questions—Implementation Team

1. What is your overall reaction to the Family Reunification Project, and the assessment and change process it calls for?

2. The primary roles of the Implementation Team were to sanction the assessment "from the top," ensure a smooth process, and promote and facilitate actual system change based on the results of the assessment. In light of these roles:

   - What is your assessment of the communication between the Implementation Team, the Management Team, and the Work Team?

   - Were there other functions the Implementation Team could have assumed?

3. How hopeful are you that real change will result from the recommendations made by the Work Team?

TIPS FOR SUCCESS

- *It is best if both the Project Director and Project Coordinator facilitate the focus groups. That way, one can ask the questions, while the other records the responses.*

- *The questions should be used only as a guide. Feel free to pursue any comments or reactions that surface.*

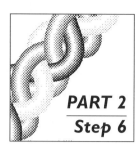

4. What could your Implementation Team do to minimize impediments and promote needed change?

5. Now that the Project is complete, are there other roles the Implementation Team might play?

Focus Group Questions—Work Team

1. Overall, how would you rate the work of this Team? What contributed most to the way the group worked together?

2. What are your reactions to the logistical aspects of the Family Reunification Project, such as

   • the meeting schedule?

   • the organization of meetings?

   • the composition of teams and the selection process?

   • the involvement of outside experts, such as school personnel?

3. In what ways did the Project Director and Project Coordinator contribute to the work of the Team?

4. Would you recommend this assessment process to other agencies? Why? Why not?

5. How hopeful are you that real change will result from the Work Team's efforts?

6. What do you see as the forces likely to promote these changes? Impede them?

7. How, if at all, has your work with this team influenced your practice?

8. What kind of involvement do you hope to have in the future in implementing the changes recommended by this assessment?

9. How would you rate the role(s) of the Implementation Team in this assessment process? What changes would you recommend with respect to this team?

10. Now that the Family Reunification Project is complete, are there other functions the Work Team might assume?

11. What other comments or suggestions do you have regarding the work of this Team?

PART 3

FRAMEWORK FOR ASSESSMENT OF STRENGTHS AND NEEDS

Introduction to the Framework and Components

I. The Agency

II. Family Reunification Services

III. Interorganizational Relations

Introduction to the
Framework and Components

The Framework for Assessment of Strengths and Needs consists of 25 components organized within the three major contexts of the family reunification system: The Agency (the child welfare agency as an organization), Family Reunification Services (the agency's family reunification services), and Interorganizational Relations (the agency's relationship to other organizations and systems).

Each Component is briefly described, followed by a set of Key Elements for Success that reflect best practice in the particular area. These Key Elements were developed in conjunction with national experts in child welfare. To help Work Team members think about the Key Elements, they should read the assigned chapters from *Together Again: Family Reunification in Foster Care* prior to each meeting. Each chapter provides material to stimulate ideas about the components. Worksheets are also provided to help conduct the assessment. Step Four of Part 2 of the *Guide,* "Conducting the Assessment" (pages 37–50), provides additional instructions on how to approach the 25 components.

The Components of Family Reunification

The first 11 components of family reunification relate to your agency's organizational structure: its purposes, personnel, and procedures. Attention to these key elements helps strengthen administrative capability. Components 12 to 16 address family reunification practice issues. Assessment and action planning in this area will result in more responsive direct services to children and their families. The final nine components focus on your agency's relationship with the "outside world." Improvements here enhance your agency's capacity to be a full member of the larger system of care.

I. The Agency

1. Mission and Principles
2. Financial Management
3. The Work Environment
4. Workloads
5. Recruitment
6. Cultural Competence
7. Social Worker Roles and Responsibilities
8. Foster Parent Roles and Responsibilities
9. Supervision
10. Staff Development
11. Program Monitoring and Evaluation

II. Family Reunification Services

12. Assessment and Goal Planning
13. Preparing Families for Reunification
14. Preparing Children for Reunification
15. Visiting
16. Postreunification Services

III. Interorganizational Relations

17. Funding Sources
18. Governmental Bodies
19. External Reviewers
20. Cross-System Collaboration
21. Court and Legal Systems
22. Community Provider Agencies
23. Law Enforcement Agencies
24. School Systems
25. Public Relations and Information

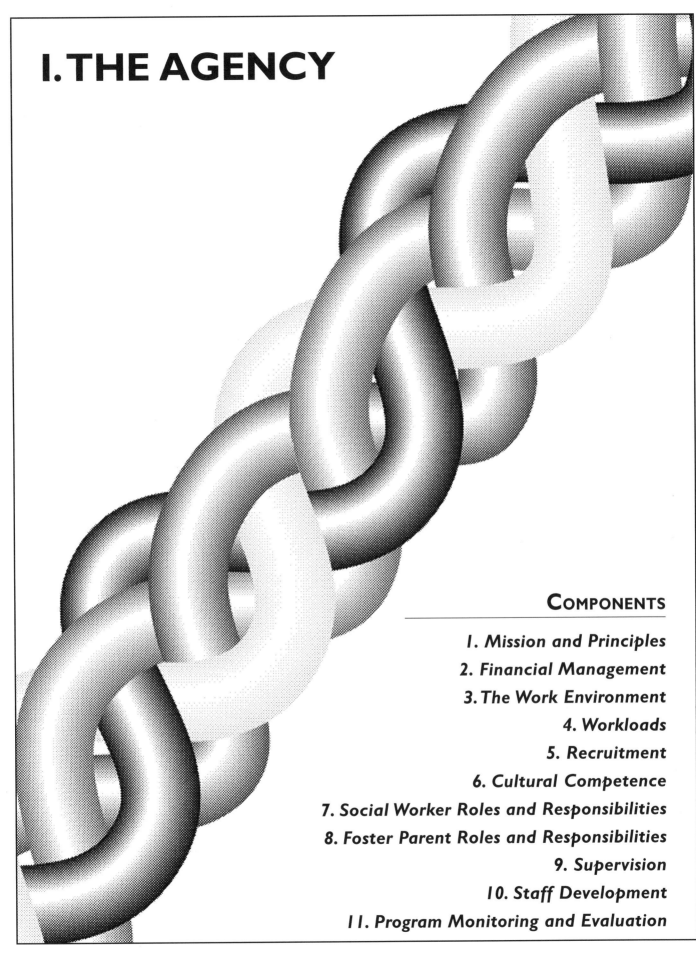

I. THE AGENCY

COMPONENTS

1. Mission and Principles
2. Financial Management
3. The Work Environment
4. Workloads
5. Recruitment
6. Cultural Competence
7. Social Worker Roles and Responsibilities
8. Foster Parent Roles and Responsibilities
9. Supervision
10. Staff Development
11. Program Monitoring and Evaluation

1. Mission and Principles

The Agency

A mission statement is a clear articulation about the reasons an organization exists, its purpose, and the principles underlying the methods through which it fulfills this purpose. A mission statement "brings clarity of focus" to all those involved in, and with, an organization.*

With respect to family reunification, it is important that the following key elements for success be incorporated into a child welfare agency's mission statement and written principles for practice.

Key Elements for Success...

A. The agency has incorporated a working definition of family reunification into its mission statement.

B. Policies and practice in family reunification are based upon a set of principles that are reflected in the mission statement, including the following:

- The biological family is the preferred child-rearing unit and is the central focus of attention.

- An adoptive or permanent foster family may be the preferred child-rearing unit in some instances. In some cases, no child-biological family contact may be sought.

- The agency respects and values the range of human diversity—ethnic, racial, cultural, religious, life-style—as well as physical and mental challenges.

- The agency views reunification as a continuum, with outcomes ranging from full reentry into the family system to less extensive contact that preserves family bonds and ensures the child's right to safety.

- Family reunification is systematically considered and, if appropriate, planned for prior to, or as early as possible following, a child's placement in out-of-home care.

- The agency provides or brokers services for as long as they are needed to maintain the reconnection through childhood and adolescence.

- Family reunification service delivery is guided by a focus on client strengths, and stresses partnership and teamwork among families and providers, including foster parents who are acknowledged as members of the service team.

continued...

---

* L. D. Goodstein, T. M. Nolan, & J. W. Pfeiffer, *Applied strategic planning: A comprehensive guide* (San Diego, CA: Pfeiffer & Co., 1992), p. 169.

The Agency

- The agency sees parents and other significant family members as vital participants in all phases of the reunification process.

- The agency regards visiting activities as an essential family reunification component. Such activities are related to the achievement of case goals, carefully planned, actively supported, and thoroughly documented.

- The agency empowers staff by providing adequate training and supervision and using the team approach in making case decisions.

1. MISSION AND PRINCIPLES

Strengths and Needs Worksheet

Directions

Review the key elements for *Component #1: Mission and Principles*, and any other related materials. Consider what elements in the agency's written documents and policies provide support for or hinder family reunification services. Note these supports (strengths) and hindrances (needs) below in preparation for the Work Team discussion. Use additional pages if necessary.

Strengths

_____

_____

_____

_____

_____

_____

_____

_____

_____

_____

_____

_____

Needs

_____

_____

_____

_____

_____

_____

_____

_____

_____

_____

_____

_____

The Agency

1. Mission and Principles

Assessment and Recommendation Worksheet

Specific Policy Needs

_____
_____
_____
_____
_____
_____
_____
_____

Specific Training Needs

_____
_____
_____
_____
_____
_____
_____
_____

Specific Resource Needs

_____
_____
_____
_____
_____
_____
_____
_____

Date: ___/___/___   Work Team: _____

2. Financial Management

The Agency

The focus of financial management should be on the critical linkages between program and fiscal staff in making decisions about allocating the resources needed to reunify families.

Key Elements for Success...

A. Program and fiscal staff jointly decide budget priorities.

B. Program staff set reunification priorities, determine need, and manage resources after budget approval. Fiscal staff do not move money without program guidance.

C. Staff can approve payment for a full range of services for both children in care and their families to expedite reunification.

D. Staff have available to them the unit costs of family support services to be purchased, and the total amounts budgeted for these services, and are thus able to make informed treatment planning decisions.

80

© 1996 CHILD WELFARE LEAGUE OF AMERICA

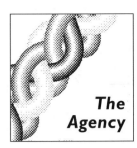
2. FINANCIAL MANAGEMENT

Strengths and Needs Worksheet

Directions

Review the key elements for *Component #2: Financial Management*, and any other related material. Consider what supports or hinders the management and allocation of funds in your agency's family reunification services. Note these supports (strengths) and hindrances (needs) below in preparation for the Work Team discussion. Use additional pages if necessary.

Strengths

_____
_____
_____
_____
_____
_____
_____
_____
_____
_____
_____
_____
_____
_____

Needs

_____
_____
_____
_____
_____
_____
_____
_____
_____
_____
_____
_____
_____

The Agency

Specific Policy Needs

_____
_____
_____
_____
_____
_____
_____
_____

Specific Training Needs

_____
_____
_____
_____
_____
_____
_____
_____

Specific Resource Needs

_____
_____
_____
_____
_____
_____
_____
_____

Date: ___/___/____   Work Team: _____

3. THE WORK ENVIRONMENT

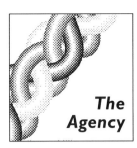

The Agency

The work environment includes all of the factors that influence how workers and others view the agency as a place in which to work. It includes tangible factors such as adequate pay, job security, benefits, health and safety standards, due process, and tools appropriate to do the work, and intangible factors such as variety and challenge; opportunities for decision making, feedback, and learning; support and respect; meaning; and opportunities for growth.*

With respect to family reunification efforts, the agency should provide a range of opportunities, resources, and supports that enhance the work environment and increase the capacity of staff members to reunify families successfully.

Key Elements for Success...

A. The agency is committed to strategic management. It involves staff at all levels, foster parents, and others in its efforts to seek new directions and pursue program improvements.

B. Staff have available to them the resources they need to reunify families, including:

- a discretionary fund (for use in meeting families' needs);

- adequate clerical and equipment supports (e.g., computerized agency forms);

- paralegal support for tasks such as sending routine letters to locate missing parents and compiling information for attorneys and the court;

- staff support (e.g., case aides) to assist with case activities such as arranging visiting and transporting parents;

- adequate space for case conferences and meetings with families; and

- adequate transportation for meetings, case conferences, and family visits.

C. Staff have the supports they need to carry out their work, including:

- adequate supervision;

- adequate training;

- support for and feedback on decision making;

- flexible work schedules to accommodate family needs; and

- adequate respite and compensatory leave.

---

*   M. R. Weisbord, *Productive workplaces: Organizing and managing for dignity, meaning, and community* (San Francisco, CA: Jossey Bass, 1991).

3. THE WORK ENVIRONMENT

Strengths and Needs Worksheet

The
Agency

Directions

Review the key elements for *Component #3: The Work Environment*, and any other related material. Consider what aspects of the work environment support or hinder your agency's family reunification services. Note these supports (strengths) and hindrances (needs) below in preparation for the Work Team discussion. Use additional pages if necessary.

Strengths

_____
_____
_____
_____
_____
_____
_____
_____
_____
_____
_____
_____
_____
_____

Needs

_____
_____
_____
_____
_____
_____
_____
_____
_____
_____
_____
_____
_____

The Agency

Specific Policy Needs

_____
_____
_____
_____
_____
_____
_____
_____

Specific Training Needs

_____
_____
_____
_____
_____
_____
_____
_____

Specific Resource Needs

_____
_____
_____
_____
_____
_____
_____
_____

Date: ___/___/____   Work Team: _____

4. Workloads

Though usually determined by the number of cases carried, workloads are better decided on the basis of the range of tasks assigned to each worker, and the time needed to complete them satisfactorily. For example, in calculating the workload of a staff member working to reunify families, consideration should be given to travel time, collateral visits, court work, family visiting and the number of family members involved, supervision and consultation, work with community groups and/or agencies, participation in staff development activities and conferences, and administrative activities such as reporting, recording, telephoning, and attending staff meetings.*

Key Elements for Success...

A. The agency follows accepted standards for caseload size.**

B. The agency has carefully considered a range of factors (case weighing) in determining a standard unit of family reunification service. These factors include family size, degree of difficulty of family problems, extent of risk factors, number of supports and services needed and used, and geographic distance.

C. The agency assigns roles and tasks in such a way that practitioners helping to reunify children and families have adequate time to carry out the wide range of activities required for competent family reunification practice.

D. The workload of individual workers is reviewed regularly and adjusted to take into account particularly difficult or demanding cases. Whenever possible, such workload adjustment is accomplished by providing extra assistance to the worker (e.g., case aides) rather than by transferring cases, which is more disruptive to families.

---

* Child Welfare League of America, *Standards for organization and administration for all child welfare services* (Washington, DC: Author, 1984).

** Although there are currently no standards for caseload size in family reunification practice, the Child Welfare League of America has set the following caseload standards: for intensive family-centered services—two to six families; for family-centered services—not to exceed 15 families; for family foster care—20 to 30 children. See Child Welfare League of America, *Standards for services to strengthen and preserve families with children* (Washington, DC: Author, 1989), and Child Welfare League of America, *Standards of excellence for family foster care* (Washington, DC: Author, 1994).

4. WORKLOADS

Strengths and Needs Worksheet

The Agency

Directions

Review the key elements for *Component #4: Workloads*, and any other related material. Consider what aspects of workload determination support or hinder your agency's family reunification services. Note these supports (strengths) and hindrances (needs) below in preparation for the Work Team discussion. Use additional pages if necessary.

Strengths

_____

_____

_____

_____

_____

_____

_____

_____

_____

_____

_____

_____

Needs

_____

_____

_____

_____

_____

_____

_____

_____

_____

_____

_____

_____

4. WORKLOADS

Assessment and Recommendation Worksheet

Specific Policy Needs

_____

_____

_____

_____

_____

_____

_____

_____

Specific Training Needs

_____

_____

_____

_____

_____

_____

_____

_____

Specific Resource Needs

_____

_____

_____

_____

_____

_____

_____

_____

Date: ___/___/____ **Work Team:** _____

5. RECRUITMENT

The Agency

Successful recruitment strategies mean that staff, volunteers, and other service providers such as foster parents are selected for their specific jobs on the basis of their personal qualities, experience, and potential for developing the attitudes and skills needed to reunify families successfully.

Key Elements for Success...

A. The agency actively recruits staff members, foster families, and volunteers who reflect the racial and ethnic composition of the families served by the agency.

B. All job descriptions delineate the qualifications of competent family reunification practitioners. Those who are hired meet these qualifications.

C. The agency advises schools of social work on curriculum development and facilitates the hiring of trained social workers.

D. The agency has apprenticeship programs to attract minority practitioners, and recruits and retains non-MSWs who can be helped to earn their degree in exchange for an agreed-upon period of service.

5. RECRUITMENT

Strengths and Needs Worksheet

The Agency

Directions

Review the key elements for *Component #5: Recruitment*, and any other related material. Consider what supports or hinders recruitment of qualified staff and foster parents for your agency's family reunification services. Note these supports (strengths) and hindrances (needs) below in preparation for the Work Team discussion. Use additional pages if necessary.

Strengths

_____

_____

_____

_____

_____

_____

_____

_____

_____

_____

_____

_____

Needs

_____

_____

_____

_____

_____

_____

_____

_____

_____

_____

_____

_____

The Agency

Specific Policy Needs

_____
_____
_____
_____
_____
_____
_____
_____

Specific Training Needs

_____
_____
_____
_____
_____
_____
_____
_____

Specific Resource Needs

_____
_____
_____
_____
_____
_____
_____
_____

Date: ___/___/____   Work Team: _____

6. CULTURAL COMPETENCE

The Agency

Cultural competence is the set of behaviors, attitudes, and policies that enable organizations and professionals to work effectively in cross-cultural situations.* In a culturally competent child welfare agency, cultural diversity is valued and incorporated at all levels—policy, administration, and service delivery.

Key Elements for Success...

A. To the extent possible, the agency's staffing pattern at all levels reflects the racial makeup of the children and families served by the agency.

B. The agency accepts and respects family styles, life-styles and child-rearing methods that might be considered different or unusual, so long as they do not endanger the child.

C. The agency seeks out advice and guidance on the delivery of family reunification services from members of the minority groups it serves.

D. The agency's efforts to help families be reunited include working in conjunction with informal helping networks within the families' own communities.

E. The agency uses intervention approaches that are congruent with the family's heritage and recognizes the ways in which cultural variables can affect assessment, goal planning, and implementation efforts.

F. The agency places children with families that help maintain and reflect the child's racial, cultural, and religious identity. Young children are placed with families who speak the same language so that language does not become an obstacle to reunification.

G. The agency is committed to developing the cultural competence of staff at all levels, especially as such competence relates to family reunification.

---

* CASSP Technical Assistance Center, Georgetown University Child Development Center, *Towards a culturally competent system of care* (vol. 1) (Washington, DC: Author, 1989).

96

6. Cultural Competence

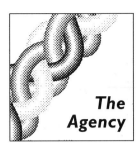

The Agency

Strengths and Needs Worksheet

Directions

Review the key elements for *Component #6: Cultural Competence*, and any other related material. Consider what supports or hinders cultural competence in your agency's family reunification services. Note these supports (strengths) and hindrances (needs) below in preparation for the Work Team discussion. Use additional pages if necessary.

Strengths

_____
_____
_____
_____
_____
_____
_____
_____
_____
_____
_____
_____
_____

Needs

_____
_____
_____
_____
_____
_____
_____
_____
_____
_____
_____
_____
_____

The Agency

Specific Policy Needs

_____
_____
_____
_____
_____
_____
_____
_____

Specific Training Needs

_____
_____
_____
_____
_____
_____
_____
_____

Specific Resource Needs

_____
_____
_____
_____
_____
_____
_____
_____
_____

Date: ___/___/____ Work Team: _____

7. Social Worker Roles and Responsibilities

The Agency

The practitioner's work with families separated by the placement of their children into family foster care is critical to the success of reunification efforts. The roles and responsibilities of the family reunification social worker must be clearly articulated in policy, and underscored and supported through training and supervision.

Key Elements for Success...

A. Reunification social workers are committed to reunification efforts that both respect family integrity and take into account the child's need for safety.

B. Reunification social workers examine and deal with their own beliefs, feelings, values, and attitudes in relation to parenting and to reunifying families, identifying in particular those that may be obstacles to reunification, such as ambivalence about reconnecting some families.

C. Reunification social workers identify those attitudes and practices that push families prematurely into reunification.

D. Reunification social workers convey to the child, the family, the foster parents, and others their commitment to reunification, even before the child is placed.

E. Reunification social workers discuss with the family, the children, and others the reasons for the original placement, what has changed and needs to change to make reunification possible, and how the family and children will be prepared for reunification.

F. Reunification social workers help foster parents cope with their feelings regarding the child's reconnection with his or her biological family and carry out tasks that support family reunification.

G. Reunification social workers arrange for immediate and consistent family contact as an essential ingredient in preparing for and maintaining a successful reunification.

H. Reunification social workers help parents to assess their ability to provide a safe, nurturing environment, helping them to identify obstacles to safety and to correct them.

I. Reunification social workers work with the family to identify the optimal level of reconnection that is possible—from actual return of child to the family to

continued...

visiting or other forms of regular contact—and help the family to recognize that the form of reconnection may need to change over time.

J. Reunification social workers develop a child's placement diary with the child's biological and foster parents, the child, and the child's teachers. The diary should reflect significant events that occurred during the placement outside of the home and should include important documents that the child would want and/or need to have.

K. Reunification social workers provide or arrange the purchase of services to help ameliorate the conditions that led to placement.

L. Reunification social workers help families advocate for needed services for themselves.

M. Reunification social workers engage in active collaboration with other providers, recognizing that family reunification practice requires the participation of numerous systems, such as legal, health, mental health, and education.

N. Reunification social workers maintain accurate and complete records of reunification service activities and of the child's and family's progress; review records with the family to determine the attainment of case goals; and revise or amend goals with the family as needed.

O. Reunification social workers hold a closing session with the family and others to summarize accomplishments, elaborate on family strengths, and review and ensure delivery of the supports that can help the family carry out the tasks ahead.

7. SOCIAL WORKER ROLES AND RESPONSIBILITIES

Strengths and Needs Worksheet

The Agency

Directions

Review the key elements for *Component #7: Social Worker Roles and Responsibilities*, and any other related material. Consider what supports or hinders social workers in carrying out their work to reunify families. Note these supports (strengths) and hindrances (needs) below in preparation for the Work Team discussion. Use additional pages if necessary.

Strengths

_____
_____
_____
_____
_____
_____
_____
_____
_____
_____
_____

Needs

_____
_____
_____
_____
_____
_____
_____
_____
_____
_____
_____

The Agency

7. SOCIAL WORKER ROLES AND RESPONSIBILITIES

Assessment and Recommendation Worksheet

Specific Policy Needs

_____
_____
_____
_____
_____
_____
_____
_____

Specific Training Needs

_____
_____
_____
_____
_____
_____
_____
_____

Specific Resource Needs

_____
_____
_____
_____
_____
_____
_____
_____

Date: ___/___/____ Work Team: _____

8. FOSTER PARENT ROLES AND RESPONSIBILITIES

The Agency

Foster parents play a central part in helping families successfully reunite. Written agency policies should delineate the foster parents' roles and responsibilities. The importance of foster parents should be evidenced in recruitment and underscored in joint training with social workers and other service providers.

Key Elements for Success...

A. The agency helps foster parents to understand, support, and demonstrate their belief in the importance of the biological family to children, and encourages foster parents to convey to children in their care their "permission" to reconnect with their families.

B. The agency encourages foster parents to identify and build on the biological family's strengths and to help meet their needs.

C. The agency values ongoing partnership among the biological family, children in care, foster parents, and other service providers.

D. The agency treats foster parents as members of the service delivery team, and provides them with adequate information about the children in their care, access to agency staff and other providers, training, and other supports in order to carry out their responsibilities in relation to family reunification.

E. Foster parents have preservice and specialized inservice training regarding their roles and their responsibility to support reunification goals for each child in their care.

F. The agency recruits foster parents from the racial and ethnic groups it serves and helps foster parents to reflect and maintain the racial, cultural, and religious identity of children in their care.

G. Foster parents have opportunities to clarify their relationship with the biological parents of the children for whom they care during and following the reunification (e.g., foster parents serve as resources by providing information about the child, new skills, empathy, and respite following the reunification).

8. FOSTER PARENT ROLES AND RESPONSIBILITIES

Strengths and Needs Worksheet

The Agency

Directions

Review the key elements for *Component #8: Foster Parent Roles and Responsibilities*, and any other related material. Consider what supports or hinders effective foster parenting in your agency's family reunification services. Note these supports (strengths) and hindrances (needs) below in preparation for the Work Team discussion. Use additional pages if necessary.

Strengths

_____

_____

_____

_____

_____

_____

_____

_____

_____

_____

_____

_____

_____

Needs

_____

_____

_____

_____

_____

_____

_____

_____

_____

_____

_____

_____

_____

The Agency

Specific Policy Needs

_____
_____
_____
_____
_____
_____
_____
_____

Specific Training Needs

_____
_____
_____
_____
_____
_____
_____
_____

Specific Resource Needs

_____
_____
_____
_____
_____
_____
_____
_____
_____

Date: ___/___/____   Work Team: _____

9. SUPERVISION

Supervision in a child welfare agency serves as a source of education, support, and assistance to providers to maximize the quality of services to families. The agency should have written guidelines for supervising social work staff that delineate methods of supervision, frequency of supervision, and content and purposes of supervisory conferences. Effective supervision is a key element in successfully reunifying families.

Key Elements for Success...

A. Supervisors receive training in—and keep abreast of—family reunification theory and practice.

B. In recognition of the challenges inherent in family reunification work, the agency gives supervisors opportunities to meet together to provide mutual support, and to work together to identify and meet their needs.

C. Supervision and consultation are individualized according to the worker's need and expertise in family reunification practices. Supervision is thus aimed at increasing practitioner competence and decreasing the need for supervision, replacing it with a consultative approach.

D. The agency has written guidelines for evaluating practitioners' performance in relation to the agency's family reunification goals and philosophy.

E. The agency helps family reunification practitioners to seek out and use supervision effectively.

F. Supervisors stay well-informed about developments in their workers' cases and actively provide case-specific guidance, including helping the worker to deal with her/his personal challenges in working on the case.

G. In recognizing that successful family reunification work is, at certain points in the process, likely to require extra time and effort, supervisors provide feedback on worker performance, especially strengths, frequently and in varied ways.

H. Practitioners regularly evaluate the degree to which the agency's supervisory arrangements meet their needs and participate in developing consultation and other forms of supervision, such as meetings with family reunification experts and peer group supervision.

9. SUPERVISION

Strengths and Needs Worksheet

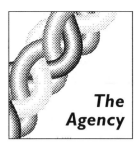

The
Agency

Directions

Review the key elements for *Component #9: Supervision*, and any other related material. Consider what supports or hinders good supervision in your agency's family reunification services. Note these supports (strengths) and hindrances (needs) below in preparation for the Work Team discussion. Use additional pages if necessary.

Strengths

_____
_____
_____
_____
_____
_____
_____
_____
_____
_____
_____
_____
_____
_____

Needs

_____
_____
_____
_____
_____
_____
_____
_____
_____
_____
_____
_____
_____

The Agency

Specific Policy Needs

_____
_____
_____
_____
_____
_____
_____
_____
_____

Specific Training Needs

_____
_____
_____
_____
_____
_____
_____
_____
_____

Specific Resource Needs

_____
_____
_____
_____
_____
_____
_____
_____
_____

Date: ___/___/____ **Work Team:** _____

10. STAFF DEVELOPMENT

The Agency

Staff development comprises the range of opportunities staff have for professional growth. These include inservice training, attendance at workshops and conferences, and leave to pursue graduate social work or related education. Providing training opportunities for foster parents, other service providers, and court personnel is a key responsibility of a child welfare agency seeking to improve the delivery of family reunification services.

Key Elements for Success...

A. The agency regularly involves staff and foster parents in assessing their family reunification training needs, planning for meeting them, and evaluating their effectiveness in achieving learning outcomes.

B. The agency provides regular inservice training in family reunification practice, with attention to staff members' and foster parents' varying levels of expertise. Opportunities for education and training are based on the individual educational goals for each staff member and foster parent.

C. Training activities model and seek to enhance partnerships and collaboration among caregivers, social workers, and other service providers.

D. Training is consistent with the agency's family reunification program goals and objectives.

E. The agency's formalized training program includes culturally competent skill-building in the following areas as they relate to family reunification: assessment, goal planning, intervention, safety planning, risk assessment, and evaluation.

F. Staff training includes the provision of current information on available services to families.

G. Training on family reunification is provided by and for attorneys and judges.

H. Staff and foster parents receive incentives and supports to participate in training.

112

10. STAFF DEVELOPMENT

Strengths and Needs Worksheet

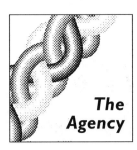

The Agency

Directions

Review the key elements for *Component #10: Staff Development,* and any other related material. Consider what supports or hinders effective staff development in your agency's family reunification services. Note these supports (strengths) and hindrances (needs) below in preparation for the Work Team discussion. Use additional pages if necessary.

Strengths

_____
_____
_____
_____
_____
_____
_____
_____
_____
_____
_____
_____
_____

Needs

_____
_____
_____
_____
_____
_____
_____
_____
_____
_____
_____
_____
_____

The Agency

Specific Policy Needs

_____
_____
_____
_____
_____
_____
_____
_____

Specific Training Needs

_____
_____
_____
_____
_____
_____
_____
_____
_____

Specific Resource Needs

_____
_____
_____
_____
_____
_____
_____
_____
_____

Date: ___/___/____ **Work Team:** _____

11. Program Monitoring and Evaluation

The
Agency

Management information systems allow child welfare agencies to collect and use a wide range of data for a number of purposes, including assessing program effectiveness, defining unmet needs and shaping new programs, formulating budgets, and being accountable to funders and the public.* Increased attention to strengthening reunification services will have implications for the agency's management information systems.

Key Elements for Success...

A. The agency has current and accurate information on all reunification services it provides, or contracts for, for the following purposes:

- to convey accurate information to policymakers, auditors, and others about numbers and levels of family reunifications achieved, and resources allocated;

- to comply with requirements of Public Law 96-272 both for an inventory of children/families served, and a management information system, in order to receive additional federal funding;

- to make informed decisions about the need to strengthen or expand family reunification services; and

- to raise questions about service delivery in order to modify current practice or policy.

B. The agency has a variety of mechanisms in place to use data that have been collected for the purposes of monitoring its family reunification programs.

C. The agency uses cost effectiveness analysis to make program decisions.

D. The agency regularly evaluates how programs are being implemented in order to improve, modify, and better manage them.

E. The agency regularly conducts both process and outcome evaluations of reunification services purchased, thus documenting not only that services were helpful, but also how effective the services were and what changes need to be considered.

F. The agency systematically evaluates the impact and outcomes of its efforts in terms of:

continued...

---

* Child Welfare League of America, *Standards for services to strengthen and preserve families with children* (Washington, DC: Author, 1989).

The Agency

- improved family relationships and caregiving;

- levels of family reconnection achieved;

- numbers of children returned home to their families;

- permanency plans for children who cannot return to their families; and

- reentry of children into placement.

G. The agency calculates its success rates on the basis of identifying and achieving families' optimal levels of reconnection, and not only on returning children home.

H. The agency aggregates the information it obtains in regular case reviews for use in program planning, evaluation and reform, and securing additional funding for family reunification services.

11. PROGRAM MONITORING AND EVALUATION

Strengths and Needs Worksheet

Directions

Review the key elements for *Component #11: Program Monitoring and Evaluation*, and any other related material. Consider what supports or hinders program monitoring and/or evaluation of your agency's family reunification services. Note these supports (strengths) and hindrances (needs) below in preparation for the Work Team discussion. Use additional pages if necessary.

Strengths

_____

_____

_____

_____

_____

_____

_____

_____

_____

_____

_____

_____

_____

Needs

_____

_____

_____

_____

_____

_____

_____

_____

_____

_____

_____

_____

11. PROGRAM MONITORING AND EVALUATION

Assessment and Recommendation Worksheet

Specific Policy Needs

_____
_____
_____
_____
_____
_____
_____
_____
_____

Specific Training Needs

_____
_____
_____
_____
_____
_____
_____
_____
_____

Specific Resource Needs

_____
_____
_____
_____
_____
_____
_____
_____
_____

Date: ___/___/____ **Work Team:** _____

II. FAMILY REUNIFICATION SERVICES

COMPONENTS

12. Assessment and Goal Planning

Services

Assessment and goal planning, both hallmarks of effective child welfare practice, are especially critical to the success of efforts to reunify families. These activities are both a product and a process that involve the family and the child in mutual decision making, occur throughout the reunification effort, and require continual monitoring and revision.

Key Elements for Success...

A. The agency assesses possibilities for reunification before, or as early as possible following, a child's placement in family foster care.

B. The agency uses an accepted protocol for assessing the risks to children of contact with their parents.

C. The agency's assessment approach respects the family's heritage and recognize that family life and child care differ among cultural groups.

D. Assessment is conducted in relation to:

- the child's and the family's willingness and readiness, to be reunited;

- the strengths, resources, and potentialities of the family and child that can make a reunion possible;

- the formal and informal resources and supports available to the family through its extended kin networks and the social service and community systems;

- the family's ability to meet the physical, social, emotional, medical, and educational needs of the child;

- the impact on the child and the family of previous experiences that led to the need for placement;

- the child's functioning and special needs;

- the level of family/child bonding, family communication patterns, and the family's conflict resolution skills;

- the family problems and safety concerns that may impede reunification; and

- the environmental obstacles that may affect reunification, including resource gaps (e.g. housing, finances, community services), attitudes and values of helpers, inadequate policies, legal procedures and requirements, and other outside pressures and stresses.

continued...

Services

E. When return home is not possible, assessment identifies the optimal level of reconnection that a child and family can be helped to make.

F. Goal planning and reviews make use of a team approach, involving all members of the reunification effort (e.g. family, foster parents, agencies, attorneys, courts, schools, family advocates), with recognition of the varying needs of these parties.

G. Goal planning takes into account the requirements of the legal system, including laws, policies, and judicial decisions.

H. Plans and service delivery are strength focused and capacity building, rather than dependency building.

I. The practitioner states attainable goals in clear terms in the family's own language and preferably using words that are most meaningful to the family. The goals emphasize behavioral changes that are related to the reasons the child was removed.

J. Goal plans spell out the roles and tasks of all participants, including in particular:

- an explanation of the goal-planning process;

- actions each participant will take in working toward the goals;

- the tasks that each participant must complete to provide for the child's growth, health, and safety, and for the family's integrity;

- small concrete tasks that can be readily achieved;

- a visiting plan that addresses ways to work on the goal of family reunification;

- a timetable, including a target date for reunification, that best reflects a child's and family's pace for goal attainment and the child's need for permanence; and

- a plan to enable the child and family to have access to services following reunion and case closure.

K. Practitioners recognize that assessment and goal planning occur throughout work with a family up to termination of the case, and that plans require continual monitoring, reassessment, and revision.

12. Assessment and Goal Planning

Strengths and Needs Worksheet

Directions

Review the key elements for *Component #12: Assessment and Goal Planning*, and any other related material. Consider what supports or hinders good assessment and goal planning in your agency's family reunification services. Note these supports (strengths) and hindrances (needs) below in preparation for the Work Team discussion. Use additional pages if necessary.

Strengths

_____

_____

_____

_____

_____

_____

_____

_____

_____

_____

_____

_____

_____

Needs

_____

_____

_____

_____

_____

_____

_____

_____

_____

_____

_____

_____

Services

Specific Policy Needs

_____
_____
_____
_____
_____
_____
_____
_____

Specific Training Needs

_____
_____
_____
_____
_____
_____
_____
_____
_____

Specific Resource Needs

_____
_____
_____
_____
_____
_____
_____
_____

Date: ___/___/____   **Work Team:** _____

13. Preparing Families for Reunification

Services

The agency should view family members—including, when appropriate, extended kin—as partners in the change process. Thus, family members need to be actively involved in preparing for reunification, including having an understanding of the reasons for placement, participating in developing goals, sharing in determining visit plans and purposes, and evaluating their own progress.

Key Elements for Success...

A. The agency helps families to understand why placement was necessary and to identify the situational factors that put their children at risk. The agency helps families learn ways of minimizing future risks to their children.

B. When a child is placed in a residential care facility, the agency helps the family to understand the reasons for placement and involves the family in developing goals and treatment plans.

C. The agency helps families to identify and accept the ways in which they and their children have changed while they were apart.

D. The agency helps families to assess the extent of their ability and willingness to reconnect with their children.

E. The agency helps families to learn parenting skills relevant to whatever level of family connection is to be achieved, including such skills as:

- arranging for their children's access to adequate food, clothing, housing, health care, education, and recreation;

- recognizing and appreciating their children's achievements;

- identifying and responding appropriately to their children's problem areas;

- helping their children to feel positive about themselves and about other family members;

- giving emotional nurturance to their children;

- providing discipline in a constructive way;

- using and interacting with community resources in behalf of their children; and

- sharing family and cultural history and values.

F. The agency engages families in a realistic assessment of their children's progress toward service goals.

continued...

G. Families participate in determining visit plans and purposes and in structuring actual visits.

H. The agency helps families to identify, understand, and appropriately respond to feelings and behaviors they might expect to see in their children following reconnection.

I. The agency helps families to identify strengths in themselves and mobilize supports in their community that can help them to maintain the reunification.

J. The agency requires that residential care facilities have active programs to involve families in preparing for a child's return.

13. Preparing Families for Reunification

Strengths and Needs Worksheet

Services

Directions

Review the key elements for *Component #13: Preparing Families for Reunification,* and any other related material. Consider what supports or hinders your agency's efforts to prepare families for reunification. Note these supports (strengths) and hindrances (needs) below in preparation for the Work Team discussion. Use additional pages if necessary.

Strengths

_____
_____
_____
_____
_____
_____
_____
_____
_____
_____
_____
_____
_____
_____
_____

Needs

_____
_____
_____
_____
_____
_____
_____
_____
_____
_____
_____
_____
_____
_____

127

Services

13. PREPARING FAMILIES FOR REUNIFICATION

Assessment and Recommendation Worksheet

Specific Policy Needs

_____
_____
_____
_____
_____
_____
_____
_____

Specific Training Needs

_____
_____
_____
_____
_____
_____
_____
_____

Specific Resource Needs

_____
_____
_____
_____
_____
_____
_____
_____

Date: ___/___/___ Work Team: _____

14. PREPARING CHILDREN FOR REUNIFICATION

The child's readiness to reunite with his/her family is critical to the success of the reunification. To the extent possible, children should be actively involved in, and their needs taken into account throughout, all aspects of the process.

Key Elements for Success...

A. Practitioners use role playing, puppet shows, storytelling, and other techniques to explain the reunification to children, including in their explanations reasons for original placement, what has already or still needs to be changed to make reconnection possible, and how the children and the family will be prepared for reunification.

B. Children are involved in the process of understanding the events that led to placement, and the decision to reunify.

C. The agency's practice with children demonstrates respect for the child's family, heritage, and history.

D. Social workers, foster parents, and child care staff help children to express their ideas about what visiting and reunification will be like and correct any misconceptions they may have.

E. Social workers, foster parents, and child care staff help children to communicate with various court personnel.

F. Social workers, foster parents, and child care staff help children to demonstrate to family members the ways in which they have changed and grown during placement.

G. When it is not possible to place siblings together, social workers, foster parents, and child care staff give attention to arranging varied and frequent sibling contact as a necessary ingredient, unless otherwise indicated, to maintaining family connections.

H. Social workers, foster parents, and child care staff help children to keep a placement diary that reflects significant events that occurred during the placement and includes important documents that their families of origin would want to have.

I. Social workers, foster parents, and child care staff help other children in the biological family who were not placed outside of the home to cope with the changes anticipated or brought on by reunification.

continued...

Services

J. Social workers, foster parents, and child care staff help children to define their wishes regarding a relationship with the foster parents following reunification, and to deal with feelings of divided loyalty toward biological and foster families.

K. Social workers, foster parents, and child care staff help children to cope with feelings that may be reactivated as departure from the foster family or residential facility approaches, such as grief, guilt, anger and fear.

L. Social workers, foster parents, and child care staff develop a safety plan with every child who has been placed because of the risk of harm; children are given opportunities to practice carrying out the plan prior to reunification.

14. PREPARING CHILDREN FOR REUNIFICATION

Strengths and Needs Worksheet

Services

Directions

Review the key elements for *Component #14: Preparing Children for Reunification*, and any other related material. Consider what supports or hinders effective preparation of children for reunification in your agency. Note these supports (strengths) and hindrances (needs) below in preparation for the Work Team discussion. Use additional pages if necessary.

Strengths

_____

_____

_____

_____

_____

_____

_____

_____

_____

_____

_____

Needs

_____

_____

_____

_____

_____

_____

_____

_____

_____

_____

_____

_____

Services

14. Preparing Children for Reunification

Assessment and Recommendation Worksheet

Specific Policy Needs

_____
_____
_____
_____
_____
_____
_____
_____

Specific Training Needs

_____
_____
_____
_____
_____
_____
_____
_____

Specific Resource Needs

_____
_____
_____
_____
_____
_____
_____
_____

Date: ___/___/___ **Work Team:** _____

15. VISITING

Visiting is the heart of all plans to reunify families. It helps maintain family ties as well as provide opportunities for family members to learn and practice new behaviors and styles of communicating. Agencies should provide and support quality visiting services that promote a child's timely return home or make possible a determination that he/she cannot return to full-time care in the family. Whether or not children are able to return home, visiting maintains family ties that are essential to a child's healthy development.*

Key Elements for Success...

A. Agencies place children near their parents and other significant family members.

B. Agencies place siblings together unless otherwise indicated.

C. Visiting environments make use, whenever possible, of natural settings, such as parks, zoos, children's museums, and the like.

D. The agency encourages foster parents to allow family visits in the foster home, unless contraindicated.

E. The agency has well-equipped, comfortable visiting rooms.

F. The agency provides flextime or compensatory time for workers so that visits can occur when families can schedule them.

G. The agency makes available to foster and biological families financial assistance for such visit-related expenses as transportation or food.

H. Staff and foster parents receive training in planning and carrying out positive visits.

I. The agency requires written visiting plans that specify visit purposes, frequency, length, location, supervision, participants, supportive services, and planned activities.

J. Children, family, foster parents, and staff participate in decisions about visiting.

K. Visiting plans balance the child's need for protection with the family's need for autonomy.

continued...

• P. M. Hess & K. O. Proch, *Family visiting in out-of-home care: A guide to practice* (Washington, DC: Child Welfare League of America, 1988).

Services

L. Visit activities are chosen by the social worker and the family that provide both children and families with opportunities to learn, practice and demonstrate new behaviors and patterns of interaction.

M. The social worker adequately prepares children, families, and foster parents for visits and gives them opportunities to work through their reactions to visits.

N. The practitioner arranges visits along a continuum of increasingly stressful times (e.g., playing in the park to mealtimes to difficult bedtimes) to help families gradually achieve competence in these areas.

O. The practitioner and the family evaluate, alter, and document the visiting plan in accordance with family and child progress and needs.

P. The practitioner and the family use visits to assess realistically whether family members have made the changes necessary to decrease the risks to the child in the home.

Q. Children are returned home only after they have safely had unsupervised visits in their own home, including overnight visits and visits lasting several days or more, over an appropriate period of time.

15. VISITING

Strengths and Needs Worksheet

Services

Directions

Review the key elements for *Component #15: Visiting*, and any other related material. Consider what supports or hinders effective visiting in your agency's family reunification services. Note these supports (strengths) and hindrances (needs) below in preparation for the Work Team discussion. Use additional pages if necessary.

Strengths

_____

_____

_____

_____

_____

_____

_____

_____

_____

_____

_____

_____

_____

Needs

_____

_____

_____

_____

_____

_____

_____

_____

_____

_____

_____

_____

Services

Specific Policy Needs

_____
_____
_____
_____
_____
_____
_____
_____
_____

Specific Training Needs

_____
_____
_____
_____
_____
_____
_____
_____
_____

Specific Resource Needs

_____
_____
_____
_____
_____
_____
_____
_____
_____

Date: ___/___/____   **Work Team:** _____

16. POSTREUNIFICATION SERVICES

Services

The services provided to a family after a child has returned home are essential in helping a family stay together. For most families, postreunification services are at first intensive, but then taper off to less frequent contact. A few families, however, may need some level of services indefinitely to maintain their children at home.

Key Elements for Success...

A. A network of supportive services that the family is comfortable using is in place prior to the reunification.

B. Agency policy is written to ensure adequate time following reunification before a case must be closed.

C. The agency has practice guidelines for ensuring the family's access to services after case termination.

D. The practitioner helps families to understand family dynamics that might include conflict and other problems, and know how to respond and when to seek help.

E. The practitioner helps families to anticipate and understand their feelings about the agency's impending departure from their lives.

F. The agency helps biological family members and foster parents to clarify their relationship following reunification (e.g., foster parents' willingness to provide respite or their availability for phone contact and visits.)

G. The agency sees respite care as an essential service to help some families stay together following their reunification. The agency has procedures in place for providing respite without reopening a protective services case (with its implication of family failure). Where possible, the agency acknowledges and supports the family's use of the foster family for respite purposes.

16. Postreunification Services

Strengths and Needs Worksheet

Services

Directions

Review the key elements for *Component #16: Postreunification Services*, and any other related material. Consider what supports or hinders the provision of post-reunification services in your agency's family reunification program. Note these supports (strengths) and hindrances (needs) below in preparation for the Work Team discussion. Use additional pages if necessary.

Strengths

_____

_____

_____

_____

_____

_____

_____

_____

_____

_____

_____

_____

_____

Needs

_____

_____

_____

_____

_____

_____

_____

_____

_____

_____

_____

_____

_____

Services

Assessment and Recommendation Worksheet

Specific Policy Needs

_____
_____
_____
_____
_____
_____
_____
_____

Specific Training Needs

_____
_____
_____
_____
_____
_____
_____
_____

Specific Resource Needs

_____
_____
_____
_____
_____
_____
_____
_____

Date: ___/___/____   Work Team: _____

III. INTERORGANIZATIONAL RELATIONS

17. Funding Sources

Gaining access to the myriad sources of funds to support their programs is a major challenge for child welfare agencies. In addition to the federal and state dollars earmarked for foster care, public agencies seeking to strengthen their family reunification services can tap categorical funding sources such as Medicaid and the Early and Periodic Screening, Diagnosis, and Treatment Program (EPSDT) and a wide range of other funded services.

Key Elements for Success . . .

A. Agency administrators are knowledgeable about federal and state funding requirements and opportunities.

B. Agency administrators prepare documentation for the governor and legislature to enable the agency to reach or maintain a level of funding adequate to support family reunification services.

C. The governor and the legislature support refinancing strategies and allocating increased federal revenue to children's services rather than to offset budget deficits.

D. The Medicaid agency and the child welfare agency jointly develop a plan to ensure that Medicaid funds are available to cover family reunification services.

E. The agency is knowledgeable about the Medicaid options included in the state's Medicaid plan.

F. The agency works with other state agencies (e.g., mental health, education) to increase funding options for reunification clients and to promote coordination of services to families (e.g., alcohol services, counseling).

G. Child welfare practitioners have access to EPSDT screening and services.

H. The agency regularly reviews alternate funding mechanisms implemented by other states.

I. The agency creates mechanisms to coordinate client eligibility across funding streams (e.g., Medicaid; Titles IV-E, IV-A, and IV-B; and SSI) that are flexible, individualized, and accessible to staff.

J. The agency makes maximum use of federal dollars to support family reunification (e.g., using Title IV-E funds to support training activities).

continued…

K. The agency works with the state to develop a plan to increase state investment in reunification services by:

- reallocating funds from institutional care;

- maximizing federal resources by sharing state cost matches across state departments; and

- establishing fiscal incentives for local jurisdictions that support reunification efforts.

17. Funding Sources

Strengths and Needs Worksheet

Interorganizational
Relations

Directions

Review the key elements for *Component #17: Funding Sources,* and any other related material. Consider what supports or hinders your agency's access to funding sources for your family reunification program. Note these supports (strengths) and hindrances (needs) below in preparation for the Work Team discussion. Use additional pages if necessary.

Strengths

_____

_____

_____

_____

_____

_____

_____

_____

_____

_____

_____

Needs

_____

_____

_____

_____

_____

_____

_____

_____

_____

_____

_____

145

17. FUNDING SOURCES

Assessment and Recommendation Worksheet

Specific Policy Needs

_____
_____
_____
_____
_____
_____
_____
_____

Specific Training Needs

_____
_____
_____
_____
_____
_____
_____
_____

Specific Resource Needs

_____
_____
_____
_____
_____
_____
_____
_____

Date: ___/___/____   Work Team: _____

18. Governmental Bodies

Interorganizational Relations

The policy framework affecting the delivery of child welfare services includes federal laws and administrative regulations, state statutes, and court decisions that involve either individual children or classes of children.* Regular and frequent communication with policymakers and those responsible for overseeing implementation is a hallmark of an effective child welfare services administration.

Key Elements for Success...

A. The agency has a designated liaison to the state legislature who is knowledgeable about permanency planning, family preservation, and the agency's philosophy about family reunification.

B. Legislators regularly have opportunities to talk with the agency's staff, clients, and foster parents; provider agencies; and court personnel about issues related to reunifying families.

C. Legislators and/or their key staff are appointed to task forces and advisory committees to deal with reunification-related issues facing the agency.

D. The agency regularly sends to policymakers and their key staff accurate and reliable information about its reunification services on which they may base their policy decisions.

E. As part of a strategic and an annual planning process, the agency identifies its program priorities for the legislature. The agency accompanies its new priority goals with accurate and realistic budget proposals that specify estimated unit costs to meet the estimated needs of family reunification clients.

F. The agency provides the legislature with options regarding choice of family reunification services, with estimates of the cost of each option.

G. The agency's relationship with staff from the regional office of the U.S. Department of Health and Human Services (HHS) (the regulatory agency) is collaborative; agency administrators look to these staff persons for consultation and technical assistance.

H. The comprehensive child welfare services plan submitted annually to HHS clearly defines goals, objectives, and programs for reunifying families.

continued...

---

* M. Allen & J. Knitzer, Child welfare: Examining the policy framework, in B. G. McGowan & W. Meezan (Eds.), *Child welfare: Current dilemmas, future directions* (Itasca, IL: F. E. Peacock, 1983).

Interorganizational Relations

I. Agency staff members regularly participate in national organizations advocating family reunification policy reform and program improvements.

J. The agency keeps abreast of significant court decisions that can inform and affect family reunification practice, including the results of relevant class action suits.

18. GOVERNMENTAL BODIES

Strengths and Needs Worksheet

Interorganizational Relations

Directions

Review the key elements for *Component #18: Governmental Bodies*, and any other related material. Consider what aspects of the policy framework support or hinder your agency's family reunification program. Note these supports (strengths) and hindrances (needs) below in preparation for the Work Team discussion. Use additional pages if necessary.

Strengths

_____

_____

_____

_____

_____

_____

_____

_____

_____

_____

_____

_____

_____

_____

Needs

_____

_____

_____

_____

_____

_____

_____

_____

_____

_____

_____

_____

_____

_____

149

Interorganizational Relations

Assessment and Recommendation Worksheet

Specific Policy Needs

_____
_____
_____
_____
_____
_____
_____
_____

Specific Training Needs

_____
_____
_____
_____
_____
_____
_____
_____

Specific Resource Needs

_____
_____
_____
_____
_____
_____
_____
_____

Date: ___/___/____ **Work Team:** _____

19. EXTERNAL REVIEWERS

Interorganizational Relations

Public Law 96-272, The Adoption Assistance and Child Welfare Act of 1980, requires that each placement of a child in family foster care be reviewed every six months. Moreover, the law sets guidelines for conducting case reviews. Some agencies use an internal review process, while others convene a citizen review board or recruit volunteers from outside the agency to review case progress.

Key Elements for Success...

A. The agency ensures that external reviewers are well-versed about the agency's mission, philosophy, policies, and priorities as they relate to family reunification.

B. The agency ensures that external reviewers receive training in permanency planning and family preservation, with particular attention to family reunification.

C. The agency ensures that external reviewers are viewed by agency staff as a valuable component in the delivery of effective family reunification services.

D. The agency ensures that external reviewers reflect the ethnic and racial backgrounds of families that receive the agency's services.

E. The agency ensures that external reviewers receive accurate information about types and availability of needed reunification services.

152

19. EXTERNAL REVIEWERS

Strengths and Needs Worksheet

Interorganizational Relations

Directions

Review the key elements for *Component #19: External Reviewers*, and any other related material. Consider what supports or hinders a good external review process in relation to your agency's family reunification program. Note these supports (strengths) and hindrances (needs) below in preparation for the Work Team discussion. Use additional pages if necessary.

Strengths

_____
_____
_____
_____
_____
_____
_____
_____
_____
_____
_____
_____
_____
_____

Needs

_____
_____
_____
_____
_____
_____
_____
_____
_____
_____
_____
_____
_____
_____

153

Interorganizational Relations

Specific Policy Needs

_____
_____
_____
_____
_____
_____
_____
_____
_____

Specific Training Needs

_____
_____
_____
_____
_____
_____
_____
_____
_____
_____

Specific Resource Needs

_____
_____
_____
_____
_____
_____
_____
_____
_____
_____

Date: ___/___/____ **Work Team:** _____

20. CROSS-SYSTEM COLLABORATION

Interorganizational Relations

Children and families working to reunify often receive services from numerous systems, including health, mental health, juvenile justice, education, and income maintenance services. Thus, the responsibility to preserve families extends far beyond the child welfare agency. To serve families effectively, child welfare agencies must plan and carry out their reunification efforts in collaboration with a broad range of service systems.*

Key Elements for Success...

A. The agency is committed to supporting a system of care that allows children and families to obtain needed family reunification services from any agency, not just child welfare.

B. The agency participates in a cross-system planning effort to allocate resources, identify service gaps, plan new services, and generate client management information data systems.

C. The agency seeks opportunities to pool its resources with other systems in order to meet the needs of children and families working to reunify (e.g., mental health systems provide screening and/or training of therapeutic foster parents; education systems provide school-based supports to children returning home from placement).

D. The agency has a cross-system case management capacity that ensures that services work together to meet the reunification needs of children and families.

E. Administrative case reviews and other case planning meetings are attended by all service providers involved with the child and family.

F. The agency collaborates with other systems to develop and implement multi-system training and staff development programs.

G. The agency collaborates with other systems to develop and use a common reunification assessment and case planning tool.

H. Parents play a strong role in all cross-system initiatives.

I. The agency has created a method for resolving cross-system conflicts that may arise.

J. Agency administrators seek support from the governor or other state leaders to mandate or otherwise promote successful cross-system collaboration.

---

* The material contained in this component was adapted from J. Knitzer & S. Yelton, Collaboration between child welfare and mental health, *Public Welfare* (Spring 1990): 24–33.

20. CROSS-SYSTEM COLLABORATION

Strengths and Needs Worksheet

Interorganizational Relations

Directions

Review the key elements for *Component #20: Cross-System Collaboration*, and any other related material. Consider what supports or hinders relationships between your agency and other systems. Note these supports (strengths) and hindrances (needs) below in preparation for the Work Team discussion. Use additional pages if necessary.

Strengths

_____
_____
_____
_____
_____
_____
_____
_____
_____
_____
_____
_____
_____
_____

Needs

_____
_____
_____
_____
_____
_____
_____
_____
_____
_____
_____
_____
_____

Interorganizational Relations

Specific Policy Needs

_____
_____
_____
_____
_____
_____
_____
_____
_____

Specific Training Needs

_____
_____
_____
_____
_____
_____
_____
_____
_____

Specific Resource Needs

_____
_____
_____
_____
_____
_____
_____
_____

Date: ___/___/____   Work Team: _____

21. Court and Legal Systems

Interorganizational Relations

In child welfare, more than in any other area of social work practice, the law asserts itself forcefully into practice.* This occurs as a result of statutes that define and fund programs, as well as a result of judges in juvenile and family courts in each state making placement and reunification decisions on a daily basis. New emphases on permanency planning for children, especially efforts to preserve and reunify families, demand that child welfare and court personnel develop collaborative relations.

Key Elements for Success...

A. All staff members in the agency are familiar with the requirements of Public Law 96-272, particularly the "reasonable efforts" clause as it relates to reunifying families. All staff are aware of the court's role in monitoring the agency's compliance with these requirements.

B. The agency has designated an expert on Public Law 96-272 (either an agency attorney or staff member who has liberal access to an attorney), to answer judges' questions and to clarify federal policy.

C. The agency advocates for, and participates in, training in permanency planning for judges, attorneys, probation officers, guardians ad litem, and others who represent children and their families.

D. The agency regularly shares with members of the judicial system its written guidelines and procedures for reunifying families, including those pertaining to service planning, documentation, visiting, and family involvement, as well as protocols for determining when reunification can no longer be considered as a viable plan.

E. In individual cases, the agency gives to the court all evidence about the services it provides to families in fulfilling its obligation to "make reasonable efforts" to reunify them.

F. The agency supports assigning a qualified and informed guardian ad litem to each child whose plan calls for reunification with his/her family. Attorneys representing the agency in judicial matters do not represent the child in care.

G. Before recommending to the court that a family be reunified, the agency convenes a case conference to determine that all relevant sources of informa-

continued...

---

* T. J. Stein, *Child welfare and the law* (New York: Longman, 1991).

tion have been consulted, guidelines for developing safety plans for children have been followed, and case goals have been achieved.

H. To assist the court in its roles relating to family reunification, the agency regularly provides information from its out-of-home care information system, especially in regard to the:

- number of children in care;

- number of families receiving family reunification services;

- types of family reunification services available and a description of them, including when they are to be used;

- family reunification services that are needed but not available;

- number of and levels of family reunifications achieved;

- number of children for whom permanency has been achieved; and

- number of children reentering placement.

I. The agency obtains legal guidance in defining what family information is to be shared with the court, and client confidentiality is defined in a way that does not unnecessarily impede the agency's collaboration with the judicial system.

J. A formal mechanism for improving agency-court relationships exists, such as a regularly convened interdisciplinary task force.

K. Agency administrators and staff are able to articulate clearly in their work with court personnel a concept of family reunification that incorporates levels of family reconnection.

L. The agency conveys to the court its support of Public Law 96-272, and lets the judge know that the agency is willing to help the court fulfill the law, through such means as:

- offering to make changes in agency forms;

- instructing agency lawyers to offer evidence in support of the findings required by federal law (e.g. "reasonable efforts");

- using agency staff to help keep tabs on compliance and to bring any problems to the court's attention;

- urging the judge to bring any procedural or personnel problems to the agency's attention and acting on them quickly; and

- responding to the judge's requests, recommendations, or orders.

M. The agency attorney:

- is present and actively represents the agency during all court hearings;

- confers with workers about cases prior to the day of each hearing;

- thoroughly plans and prepares for contested hearings and has face-to-face conferences with the social worker at least two days in advance;

- maintains regular office hours at the agency (to be available to talk with staff);

- meets periodically with the agency (e.g., at least once per year) to make sure that each case is legally on track;

continued...

Interorganizational Relations

- trains staff about legal issues and the court;

- always obtains agency permission before reaching settlements;

- helps to develop local forms for agency reports and court orders;

- helps to obtain favorable court procedures, forms, and rules at the state level by working with the Administrative Office of the Courts, Supreme Court, or Court Rules Committee; and

- helps to ensure that the agency's regulations and policy manual are consistent with federal laws and regulations as well as state statutes.

N. The child welfare agency and the juvenile court have a jointly developed written policy regarding procedures for dealing with cases they share (i.e., "children in need of supervision" cases). Probation officers and child welfare staff work cooperatively to help children and youths to be reunified with their families as soon as possible, if placement cannot be avoided.

162

21. COURT AND LEGAL SYSTEMS

Strengths and Needs Worksheet

Interorganizational
Relations

Directions

Review the key elements for *Component #21: Court and Legal Systems*, and any other related material. Consider what supports or hinders relations between your agency and the judicial system with respect to reunifying families. Note these supports (strengths) and hindrances (needs) below in preparation for the Work Team discussion. Use additional pages if necessary.

Strengths

_____
_____
_____
_____
_____
_____
_____
_____
_____
_____
_____
_____
_____

Needs

_____
_____
_____
_____
_____
_____
_____
_____
_____
_____
_____
_____

Interorganizational Relations

Assessment and Recommendation Worksheet

Specific Policy Needs

_____
_____
_____
_____
_____
_____
_____
_____

Specific Training Needs

_____
_____
_____
_____
_____
_____
_____
_____

Specific Resource Needs

_____
_____
_____
_____
_____
_____
_____
_____

Date: ___/___/___   **Work Team:** _____

22. Community Provider Agencies

Interorganizational
Relations

Child welfare agencies typically purchase a wide range of services to supplement those they are able to provide directly to children and families. Successfully reunifying families often means purchasing clinical services, parenting classes, supervised visiting, parent aide services, and other supports family reunification practitioners need to provide to help families achieve case goals.

Key Elements for Success...

A. The agency makes clear to all provider agencies its mission, philosophy, and policies about family reunification and permanency planning.

B. The agency has a mechanism to ensure that practitioners can convey information about needed services to program planners and decision makers.

C. Contracts for services explicitly detail the services to be provided and the client outcomes to be achieved in order for families to be reunited.

D. Staff from community provider agencies regularly participate in exchanges with staff and families in the child welfare agency for purposes of problem-solving, service planning, program evaluation, and training.

E. Agency staff are given clear responsibilities with respect to obtaining and coordinating needed community services.

F. The agency has a procedure in place to allow its staff to purchase emergency services outside the agency when necessary.

G. When families are separated because a child needs residential placement, staff in the facility work with the family reunification practitioner and the family on a plan to help ensure the child's reunification.

H. The agency assures the monitoring of and accountability for purchased services by having agency staff and clients regularly participate in evaluating the services to which reunification clients are referred.

22. COMMUNITY PROVIDER AGENCIES

Strengths and Needs Worksheet

Interorganizational Relations

Directions

Review the key elements for *Component #22: Community Provider Agencies*, and any other related material. Consider what supports or hinders relations between your agency and its provider agencies with respect to reunifying families. Note these supports (strengths) and hindrances (needs) below in preparation for the Work Team discussion. Use additional pages if necessary.

Strengths

_____
_____
_____
_____
_____
_____
_____
_____
_____
_____
_____
_____

Needs

_____
_____
_____
_____
_____
_____
_____
_____
_____
_____
_____

Interorganizational Relations

22. COMMUNITY PROVIDER AGENCIES

Assessment and Recommendation Worksheet

Specific Policy Needs

_____
_____
_____
_____
_____
_____
_____
_____

Specific Training Needs

_____
_____
_____
_____
_____
_____
_____
_____

Specific Resource Needs

_____
_____
_____
_____
_____
_____
_____
_____

Date: ___/___/____ **Work Team:** _____

23. Law Enforcement Agencies

Interorganizational Relations

Staff in child welfare agencies and police and probation officers are often jointly involved in cases. These cases are usually those in which families are experiencing the most difficult problems, such as family violence or sexual abuse. Officers and social workers may come into conflict over how best to proceed, in light of the competing organizational goals of crime prevention and family preservation. Further, law enforcement personnel exposed to the most challenging of family problems may feel that such problems are intractable and thus find it difficult to support the reunification of families already seen as "failures." The support of law enforcement agencies, however, may be critical in helping a family that is reunified to stay together.

Key Elements for Success...

A. The agency makes known to law enforcement agencies its federal mandate to reunify families, and its mission and philosophy on family reunification.

B. The agency has cooperative agreements with law enforcement agencies that:

- clarify the respective roles and responsibilities of law enforcement and child welfare personnel in relation to family reunification;

- provide for regular joint training sessions on family crisis, violence, child protection, and the impact of separation from family on children;

- define a protocol for responding to family crises; and

- prohibit removal of a child from her/his family without communication and collaboration with the child welfare agency.

170

23. LAW ENFORCEMENT AGENCIES

Strengths and Needs Worksheet

Interorganizational
Relations

Directions

Review the key elements for *Component #23: Law Enforcement Agencies*, and any other related material. Consider what supports or hinders good relations with law enforcement agencies with respect to reunifying families. Note these supports (strengths) and hindrances (needs) below in preparation for the Work Team discussion. Use additional pages if necessary.

Strengths

_____

_____

_____

_____

_____

_____

_____

_____

_____

_____

_____

_____

_____

Needs

_____

_____

_____

_____

_____

_____

_____

_____

_____

_____

_____

_____

171

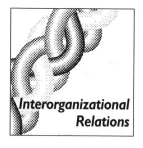

Interorganizational Relations

Specific Policy Needs

_____
_____
_____
_____
_____
_____
_____
_____

Specific Training Needs

_____
_____
_____
_____
_____
_____
_____
_____
_____

Specific Resource Needs

_____
_____
_____
_____
_____
_____
_____
_____
_____

Date: ___/___/____ Work Team: _____

24. School Systems

Schools are an integral part of the system of social services to children and families. Child protection reports frequently come from school personnel, and the majority of children in the child welfare system have special educational needs that schools are mandated to meet. In order to help reunify families that have been separated by a child's placement, either in a family foster home or a residential facility, child welfare and school personnel must work collaboratively.

Key Elements for Success...

A. The agency makes known to school systems its federal mandate to reunify families and its philosophy and practices with respect to family reunification.

B. The agency collaborates with the school to plan for the education of children with special needs who are in family foster care.

C. The agency involves parents in planning for their children's education whenever possible.

D. Foster parents participate in developing educational plans for children in their care.

E. When children are placed in residential care, the agency requires that, in planning for the child's return home, staff in the treatment facility meet with school officials in the child's home community to plan for the child's transition to the local school.

24. School Systems

Strengths and Needs Worksheet

Interorganizational Relations

Directions

Review the key elements for *Component #24: School Systems*, and any other related material. Consider what supports or hinders good relations with your local school systems in relation to reunifying families. Note these supports (strengths) and hindrances (needs) below in preparation for the Work Team discussion. Use additional pages if necessary.

Strengths

_____
_____
_____
_____
_____
_____
_____
_____
_____
_____
_____
_____
_____

Needs

_____
_____
_____
_____
_____
_____
_____
_____
_____
_____
_____
_____
_____

24. SCHOOL SYSTEMS

Assessment and Recommendation Worksheet

Specific Policy Needs

_____
_____
_____
_____
_____
_____
_____
_____
_____

Specific Training Needs

_____
_____
_____
_____
_____
_____
_____
_____

Specific Resource Needs

_____
_____
_____
_____
_____
_____
_____

Date: ___/___/____ **Work Team:** _____

25. PUBLIC RELATIONS AND INFORMATION

Interorganizational Relations

Child welfare agencies are in the public trust and are often seen as the protectors of children. Failure, as in the case of a tragic death or gross abuse, usually receives much public attention. A successful child welfare agency takes a proactive stance in communicating to the public its purposes, challenges, and successes through a variety of methods, including hosting public meetings and open houses, maintaining a speaker's bureau, publishing an in-house newsletter, and establishing contacts with the print and broadcast media. Since family reunification in cases where families have already experienced significant problems are often the riskiest in terms of child safety, both actual and perceived, a comprehensive plan for public relations is needed.

Key Elements for Success...

A. The agency has appointed a knowledgeable spokesperson to serve as liaison to the media in relation to family reunification.

B. The agency works to develop collaborative relationships with print and broadcast media that are ongoing and aim to educate the public about reunification issues.

C. The agency has guidelines for reporting to the media on reunification, particularly the most challenging, and sometimes least successful, cases.

D. The agency encourages its staff to participate in community events that provide opportunities for educating the public in relation to family reunification.

25. PUBLIC RELATIONS AND INFORMATION

Strengths and Needs Worksheet

Interorganizational Relations

Directions

Review the key elements for *Component #25: Public Relations and Information*, and any other related material. Consider what supports or hinders good publicity about your agency's family reunification services. Note these supports (strengths) and hindrances (needs) below in preparation for the Work Team discussion. Use additional pages if necessary.

Strengths

_____
_____
_____
_____
_____
_____
_____
_____
_____
_____
_____
_____
_____

Needs

_____
_____
_____
_____
_____
_____
_____
_____
_____
_____
_____
_____
_____
_____

25. PUBLIC RELATIONS AND INFORMATION

Assessment and Recommendation Worksheet

Specific Policy Needs

_____
_____
_____
_____
_____
_____
_____
_____

Specific Training Needs

_____
_____
_____
_____
_____
_____
_____
_____

Specific Resource Needs

_____
_____
_____
_____
_____
_____
_____
_____

Date: ___/___/____ **Work Team:** _____

PART 4

ANNOTATED
BIBLIOGRAPHY

SUMMARY

This section contains an annotated bibliography to help you conduct the Family Reunification Project and make needed improvements in your family reunification services. The abstracts of articles and books are organized into the following sections:

I. Family Reunification (General)

II. Improving Work and Workplaces

III. Program Monitoring and Evaluation

IV. Enhancing Cultural Competence

V. Staff Development and Training

VI. Working with the Legal System

VII. Funding Services and Programs

VIII. Working with Children and Families

182

I. FAMILY REUNIFICATION (GENERAL)

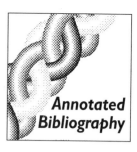

Abramczyk, L. W., & Ross, J. W. (1993). *International Reunification Symposium.* Columbia, SC: University of South Carolina, College of Social Work, The Center for Child and Family Studies.

> This collection of papers presented at a symposium on family reunification focuses on new directions in permanency planning and family preservation, recent research on family foster care and group care, and strategies for achieving and maintaining family reunification.

Ahart, A., Bruer, R., Rutsch, C., Schmidt, R., & Zaro, S. (1992). *Final report: Intensive foster care reunification programs.* Washington, DC: U.S. Department of Health and Human Services, Planning and Evaluation, Macro International Inc.

> This study of nine programs around the country provides clear and concise information on all aspects of program planning and implementation in family reunification. Extremely helpful for agencies seeking to develop new efforts or to revamp their existing programs, the report contains details on program evaluation and samples of forms and outlines used by the programs studied.

Berrick, J. D., Barth, R. P., & Needell, B. (1994). A comparison of kinship foster homes and family foster homes: Implications for kinship foster care as family preservation. *Children and Youth Services Review, 16*(1/2), 33–63.

> This study examines the characteristics of kinship foster parents and clarifies the differences between them and nonrelative foster parents, with particular regard to age, gender, income, health, race, and ethnicity. It found that regular contact between children and biological parents was more common in kinship foster families than in nonrelative foster families, and that reunification rates were lower for kinship placements.

Cahn, K., & Johnson, P. (Eds.). (1993). *Children can't wait: Reducing delays for children in out-of-home care.* Washington, DC: Child Welfare League of America.

> This book presents various approaches used by state agencies to reduce drift of children in out-of-home care and expedite decision making so that children can return to their families or be placed permanently with other families in a timely fashion. Highlighted are strategies that agencies can use to improve outcomes for children, such as advocating for changes in laws and administrative codes, promoting interagency collaboration, and increasing resources to support children in out-of-home care and their families.

Davis, I. P., English, D. J., & Landsverk, J. A. (1993). *Going home—and returning to care: A study of foster care reunification.* San Diego, CA: San Diego State University, College of Health and Human Services, School of Social Work, and The Child and Family Research Group.

> This is an extensive, longitudinal study of a cohort of reunified foster children 12 years of age or younger from public agencies in southern California and Washington State. Preliminary findings show complex associations among

child and family characteristics, service delivery variables, and reunification outcomes. As with other studies, this one provides only partial answers to such questions as (1) How do successfully reunited children differ from those requiring re-referral to child protection agencies following reunification?; and (2) What distinguishes children who are reunified from those for whom permanency planning involves adoption, guardianship, or long-term family foster care?

Hubbell, R., Hirsch, G., Barrett, B., Condelli, L., & Plantz, M. (1986). *Evaluation of reunification for minority children.* Washington, DC: U.S. Department of Health and Human Services, Office of Human Development Services, Administration for Children, Youth and Families and CRS Incorporated (Contract no. 105–84–1803).

A study of eight child welfare agencies' efforts to reunify minority children in out-of-home care with their families found a number of factors to be associated with successful and early return, including frequent case reviews, amount of caseworker time spent with families, frequency of family contacts and visiting, training of staff, racial similarity of staff and families, involvement of families in case planning, and involvement of foster parents on the treatment team. The lack of suitable housing was a significant factor in keeping families from being reunified.

Katz, L. (1990). Effective permanency planning for children in foster care. *Social Work, 35,* 220–226.

This article describes a model program that combined administrative and casework components to achieve permanency planning for young children who had been abused or seriously neglected. Approaches included reducing caseloads, early case planning, contracting with parents, providing intensive services, and emphasizing parental visiting. In addition, foster-adoptive placements were sought to eliminate unnecessary moves for children whose status might change from family foster care to adoption, with an emphasis on open adoption, allowing for biological parent contact after legalization. These approaches were coupled with administrative changes that integrated the agency's separate out-of-home care and adoption units and merged legal and social case planning.

Knitzer, J., & Yelton, S. (1990). Collaborations between child welfare and mental health. *Public Welfare, 48*(2),24–33.

The increasingly complex problems faced by troubled children and their families, including those on the path to reunification, place the child welfare and mental health systems under great pressure. One result has been a growing interest in cross-system collaboration. The authors examine the basis for this new interest; highlight some emerging collaborations, particularly in the area of family preservation; present the four obstacles that typically obstruct the implementation of cross-system initiatives; and suggest a range of strategies for overcoming those obstacles.

Maluccio, A. N., Fein, E., & Davis, I. P. (1994). Family reunification: Research findings, issues, and directions. *Child Welfare, 73,* 489–504.

The authors review research findings from studies pertaining to family reunification of children and youths in out-of-home care; delineate knowledge gaps and issues that should be explored through research; and identify emerging research priorities. Studies completed thus far provide only partial answers to such crucial questions as: How do successfully reunified families differ from these requiring referral back to child protection services? What distinguishes

children who are reunified with their families of origin from those for whom permanency planning involves adoption, guardianship, or long-term out-of-home care? How can reunified families best be helped to maintain the reunification?

Maluccio, A. N., Fein, E., & Olmstead, K. A. (1986). *Permanency planning for children: Concepts and methods.* New York and London: Routledge, Chapman and Hall.

Basic text on the theory and practice of permanency planning for children and youth who come to the attention of the child welfare system. There is emphasis on practice principles and strategies for reuniting children in foster care with their families when appropriate.

Pine, B.A., Warsh, R., & Maluccio, A. N. (Eds). (1993). *Together again: Family reunification in foster care.* Washington, DC: Child Welfare League of America.

This volume brings together a variety of in-depth perspectives on the specialized and focused practice of family reunification. Each of its 11 chapters, with contributions from nationally recognized experts in child welfare, addresses a particular aspect of family reunification and suggests principles and strategies to guide the work of providers. The book is divided into three parts. Part One, "Creating the Context," presents an overview of family reunification, strategies for building court-agency partnerships, issues related to staff training, and the features of a community mental health center that support family reunification work. Part Two, "Creating the Methods," focuses on goal setting with families, reunification from a residential setting, visiting, preparing children for reunification, and the importance of believing in families. Part Three, "Creating the Knowledge Base," addresses evaluation and the interaction of research and practice in family reunification.

II. Improving Work and Workplaces

Adams, J. (Ed.). (1984). *Transforming work: A collection of organizational transformation readings.* Alexandria, VA: Miles River Press.

Organizational transformation is among the newest thrusts for improving performance in the workplace. Although still an incomplete concept, it attempts to focus on the comprehensive changes that organizations will need to make in order to solve the problems and survive the challenges they face. The book, with 18 chapters contributed by leaders in the field of organization development and system change, is informative and helpful to administrators. It provides an overview of the concept, explores the leader's role in organizational transformation, and provides examples of the processes in action.

Bradford, L. P. (1976). *Making meetings work: A guide for leaders and group members.* San Diego, CA: University Associates.

As the title suggests, this helpful little book provides a wealth of information and resources for leading and participating in work groups. There are chapters on topics such as leadership, group dynamics, dysfunctional behavior, and planning for work group conferences. Appendixes include a number of assessment tools for evaluating group process and effectiveness.

Francis, D., & Young, D. (1992). *Improving work groups: A practical manual for team building.* San Diego, CA: Pfeiffer and Co.

The use of work teams is one of the most flexible and effective approaches to the multiple challenges faced by agencies in today's increasingly demanding environment. Teams or work groups are usually highly motivated, own the processes of problem solving and its outcomes, build collective strength, and make better quality decisions. This book is an excellent resource for team building and development. Several introductory chapters provide an overview of the use of teams and team building. The heart of the book consists of chapters that are organized around the 12 characteristics of an effective team, and how to assess and achieve them. Team exercises for strengthening all of these aspects of teamwork are carefully detailed.

Spencer, L. J. (1989). *Winning through participation: Meeting the challenge of corporate change with the technology of participation.* Dubuque, IA: Kendall/Hunt.

Although aimed at the corporate sector, this is a useful book for child welfare administrators as well as it tells how to transform participative management theory into practice. The rationale for and benefits of employee participation in decision making are well developed and an entire section is devoted to carrying out participatory techniques, with directions, examples, and illustrations.

Annotated Bibliography

Weisbord, M. R. (1991). Productive workplaces: Organizing and managing for dignity, meaning, and community. San Francisco: Jossey-Bass.

"Permanent whitewater" is how Weisbord characterizes the environment of today's organizations. Such an environment demands new forms of data collection, problem solving, and planning. This book integrates histories, theories, and methods from leaders in management innovation with examples of new organizational processes drawn from the author's extensive practice. The author provides guidelines and instructions for involving people cooperatively in designing work environments and creating organizational change.

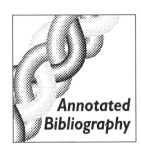

Child Welfare League of America. *Standards*. Washington, DC: Author (various publication dates).

Setting standards for quality practice has been a major goal of the Child Welfare League of America (CWLA) since its formation in 1920. In developing standards for practice, CWLA follows a systematic process of reviewing current knowledge about practice and child development, studying current research in social work and other fields, and consulting with national experts and representatives of the practice community. Currently there are volumes of standards in 11 child welfare service areas. Each volume can be used to examine an agency's practice and evaluate its adequacy in the particular area. All volumes are indexed and cross-referenced. Of particular relevance to agencies seeking to evaluate and strengthen their family reunification efforts are the following volumes:

- *CWLA Standards of Excellence for Foster Family Care*

- *CWLA Standards of Excellence for Residential Group Care Services*

- *CWLA Standards for Service for Abused and Neglected Children and Their Families*

- *CWLA Standards for Services to Strengthen and Preserve Families with Children*

- *CWLA Standards for In-Home Aide Services for Children and Their Families*

- *CWLA Standards for Health Care Services for Children in Out-of-Home Care*

- *CWLA Standards for Organization and Administration for all Child Welfare Services* (the basic companion volume for all of the programmatic standards)

Fein, E., & Staff, I. (1993). The interaction of research and practice in family reunification. In B. A. Pine, R. Warsh, & A. N. Maluccio (Eds.), *Together again: Family reunification in foster care* (pp. 199–212). Washington, DC: Child Welfare League of America.

Following a concise overview of practice-oriented research, the authors depict the potential benefits of embarking on research in family reunification programs. A study of the reunification project of a private child welfare agency is used as illustration, preliminary findings are presented, and implications for policy and practice are discussed.

Finch, S., Fanshel, D., & Grundy, J. (1991). *Data collection in adoption and foster care*. Washington, DC: Child Welfare League of America.

This book focuses on the nature and uses of management information systems (MIS) in child welfare agencies. The authors emphasize recent technological advances such as new approaches to data collection and the use of expert systems to enhance decision making, especially in out-of-home care and

adoption. Essential elements of an effective MIS are delineated, and practical information for administrators on meeting the reporting requirements of Public Law 96-272 is provided.

Finch, S., Fanshel, D., & Grundy, J. (1987). Factors associated with the discharge of children from foster care. *Social Work Research & Abstracts, 10–18.*

The authors have developed a methodology for monitoring the variables associated with discharge of children from out-of-home care in New York City, using data from a computerized management information system that has been tracking children in care for almost a decade. In essence, they apply analytic techniques used in accounting to the discharge of children from care, utilizing as predictors demographic variables describing the child, structural variables such as the child's length of time in care, discharge goals, reason-for-placement variables, and characteristics of the agency that placed the child. This methodology is useful in tracking children in out-of-home care and can be expanded to include other variables such as visiting, which would in turn provide additional information about the structure of the out-of-home care system.

Gustafson, L., & Allen, D. (1994. A new management model for child welfare: True reform means doing things differently. *Public Welfare, 52*(1), 31–40.

The authors propose a framework for improved management of child welfare agencies. Though not specifically focused on family reunification services, the framework highlights pertinent considerations in areas such as mission statements, service activities, and performance standards.

Hess, P. M., Folaron, G., & Jefferson, A. B. (1992). Effectiveness of family reunification services: An innovative evaluative model. *Social Work, 37,* 304–311.

This article describes the implementation of the Professional Review Action Group (PRAG) model for reviewing cases of disrupted family reunification. The PRAG model provides for care reviews, periodic reporting of review findings (a feedback mechanism for the agency and community), and recommendations for —and documentation of—corrective actions. In the first 62 cases reviewed, both family and service delivery problems were found to contribute directly to placement reentry. The most frequent contributor to placement reentry was nonresolution of the parental problems that precipitated placement. Multiple service delivery system problems, including large caseloads, staff turnover, and insufficient regulation of reunification practice, interacted with the serious nature of families' problems to reduce the chances for successful reunification. The authors describe a range of corrective actions to help alleviate said problems, make recommendations for resolving problems related to caseload size and staff turnover, and conclude that the PRAG model provides an effective tool for understanding and addressing undesirable policy, program, and practice outcomes in family reunification.

Hubbell, R., Hirsch, G., Barrett, B., Condelli, L., & Plantz, M. (1986). *Evaluation of reunification for minority children.* Washington, DC: U.S. Department of Health and Human Services, Office of Human Development Services, Administration for Children, Youth and Families and CRS Incorporated (Contract # 105–84–1803).

The authors use the methodology of "system dynamic modeling" to investigate the interaction between agencies and minority children and their families involved in out-of-home care in eight child welfare agencies in four states. This methodology facilitates the examination of numerous factors affecting an agency's capacity to reunify minority children with their families. The researchers examined the case records of over 700 children and interviewed over 700

Annotated Bibliography

agency administrators as well as 75 family members. Findings indicated that agency policies and practices significantly affect reunification rates, as well as the time required for reunification in cases involving minority children. There was a positive correlation between reunification rates and factors such as placement with "model" foster parents, worker contacts with other agencies on behalf of the family, and caseworker time spent with the family. In particular, the authors found that it is essential that agencies keep biological parents motivated and involved in case plans and activities in order to promote the child's return home.

Staff, I., & Fein, E. (1994). Inside the black box: An exploration of service delivery in a family reunification program. *Child Welfare, 73,* 195–211.

This evaluation of a family reunification program in a voluntary agency documents the importance of examining the process as well as outcomes of services. Suggestions for the study of process in such a setting are offered and practical illustrations are provided.

Turner, J. (1993). Evaluating family reunification programs. In B. A. Pine, R. Warsh, & A. N. Maluccio (Eds.) *Together again: Family reunification in foster care* (pp. 179–198). Washington, DC: Child Welfare League of America.

The author encourages practitioners to consider program evaluation as an essential component of family reunification practice. Strategies for undertaking an evaluation are described, along with examples of current evaluation efforts in selected family reunification programs.

192

IV. Enhancing Cultural Competence

Annotated Bibliography

CAASP Technical Assistance Center, Georgetown University Child Development Center. (1989). *Towards a culturally competent system of care: Volume I—A monograph on effective services for minority children who are severely emotionally disturbed.* Washington, DC: Author.

> This monograph defines cultural competence and provides a philosophical framework as well as practical ideas for improving service delivery to children of color. Although focused on services to children with emotional problems, the material can be easily adapted to other service areas.

CAASP Technical Assistance Center, Georgetown University Child Development Center. (1991). *Towards a culturally competent system of care: Volume II—Programs which utilize culturally competent principles.* Washington, DC: Author.

> While Volume I (above) posits the concept of cultural competence as a developmental process and a goal toward which agencies can strive, Volume II shows cultural competence in action by examining 11 programs around the country. The programs were selected from a national survey of 98 agencies providing services to emotionally disturbed children from at least one major ethnic minority group. Readers can find strategies for integrating the valuing of diversity in all aspects of their programs, from providing direct services to policymaking.

Castex, G. M. (1994). Providing services to Hispanic/Latino populations: Profiles in diversity. *Social Work, 39*, 288–296.

> Given that Hispanics come from 26 nations, the designation "Hispanic" might be regarded as confusing at best. This article provides a set of practice guidelines to help the practitioner respond to the Hispanic client's ethnic self-identity along the following features: national origin, language, family names, racial ascription, religion, self-ascription, and immigration or citizenship status.

Child Welfare League of America. (1993). *Cultural competence self-assessment instrument.* Washington, DC: Author.

> This manual is designed to promote cultural competence in the design and delivery of child welfare services. It contains an instrument for assessing an agency's strengths and weaknesses in incorporating and valuing cultural diversity at all levels of the organization—governance, policymaking, procedural, and practice. Suggestions are provided for carrying out the assessment and interpreting and using the results.

Dillon, D. (1994). Understanding and assessment of intragroup dynamics in family foster care: African American families. *Child Welfare, 73*, 129–139.

> The author stresses that assessment, case planning, and treatment in child welfare practice with African American families require a profound intracultural understanding. He considers, in particular, how ethnic identity, social class, and cultural values affect the provision of clinical services in family foster care.

193

Annotated Bibliography

Everett, J. E., Chipungu, S. S., & Leashore, B. (1991). *Child welfare: An Africentric perspective.* New Brunswick, NJ: Rutgers University Press.

This comprehensive text examines the special needs and qualities of African American children, youths, and families involved with the child welfare system. Especially valuable is the authors' emphasis on the strengths inherent in the functioning of African American families and the development of African American children and youths.

Folaron, G., & Hess, P. M. (1993). Placement considerations for children of mixed African American and Caucasian parentage. *Child Welfare, 72,* 113–125.

Based on results of their study of 62 children who reentered care after reunification, which showed that a disproportionate number of them were biracial, Folaron and Hess undertook a case-by-case analysis to determine why. They found that children who were of mixed racial parentage entered care at a younger age than those who were not, often because the Caucasian mother's family had urged that the child be placed in care. They also found that parents were ambivalent about their child's race and in some cases denied the mixed racial heritage. In none of the cases studied were services provided that helped parents or children to deal with racial issues. Moreover, there was minimal attention paid to whether the foster placement was appropriate given the child's dual heritage. The authors offer recommendations for improved permanency planning for children whose biological parents are both African American and Caucasian. They provide criteria for making placements that are sensitive to a child's identity, and value and preserve his or her dual cultural heritage. The criteria are reproduced in the "Resources" section of this book.

Ho, M. K. (1992). *Minority children and adolescents in therapy.* Newbury Park, CA: Sage Publications.

This comprehensive text focuses on clinical assessment and treatment of children and youths from Asian and Pacific American, American Indian and Alaskan native, Hispanic American, and African American backgrounds. It includes culture-specific methods, techniques, and skills for individual therapy, family therapy, and group therapy with clients from these groups.

Hogan, P. T. & Siu, S. F. (1988). Minority children in the child welfare system: An historical perspective. *Social Work, 33,* 493–498.

Following a review of the historical treatment of minority children in the child welfare system, the authors consider strategies for making the system more responsive to the needs of African American, Hispanic, and Native American children and their families.

Olsen, L. (1982) Services for minority children in out-of-home care. *Social Services Review, 56,* 572–585.

Using data from an extensive national study of public social services for children and their families, the author compares African American, Hispanic, Asian, and Native American children on such service dimensions as case planning and permanency planning. The findings show that the needs of minority children and their families have been neglected by the child welfare system. Recommendations are offered for correcting this problem for each of the above groups.

Pinderhughes, E. E. (1991). The delivery of child welfare services to African American clients. *American Journal of Orthopsychiatry, 61,* 598–605.

This paper examines the importance of cultural awareness in child welfare settings, especially in relation to decisions about maintaining children in their own homes, placing them in out-of-home care, and reunifying them with their families. The implications of such awareness for practice, administration, and policy formulation are also considered.

V. Staff Development and Training

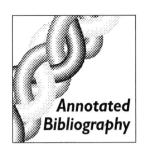

Hughes, R. C. & Rycus, J. S. (1989). *Target: Competent staff—Competency-based inservice training for child welfare.* Washington, DC: Child Welfare League of America and Institute for Human Services.

> Competency-based training is an approach in which worker performance and practice outcomes are tied to agency goals and a supportive agency context. This concise monograph presents the structure and components of a competency-based inservice training system in child welfare and provides guidance in establishing such a system. Core and specialized competencies for direct practice in child welfare are delineated.

Pine, B. A., Warsh, R., & Maluccio, A. N. (1993). Training for competence in family reunification practice. In B. A. Pine, R. Warsh, & A. N. Maluccio (Eds.), *Together again: Family reunification in foster care* (pp. 35–50). Washington, DC: Child Welfare League of America.

> The authors describe a competency-based approach to educating and training agency staff in which performance and practice outcomes are tied to agency goals and to a supportive agency context. They identify the knowledge, attitudes, and skills needed for family reunification practice, and include a sampling of training activities that illustrate the competency-based approach.

University of South Carolina, College of Social Work, The Center for Family Studies. (1993). *Foster care reunification: A training package for child welfare workers involved in permanency planning.* Columbia, SC: Author.

> This comprehensive and systematic training package was extensively field tested with three pilot groups of public and private child welfare workers from more than half of South Carolina's 46 counties. The package includes curriculum materials for a five-day course focusing on family reunification. There is careful delineation of course objectives, content, and methods, with emphasis on such aspects as child development and family systems theories, along with their significance for assessment, case planning, case management, and family treatment in out-of-home care situations.

Warsh, R., Maluccio, A. N., & Pine, B. A. (1994). *Teaching family reunification: A sourcebook.* Washington, DC: Child Welfare League of America.

> The *Sourcebook* is a four-part resource for training and educating child welfare personnel about family reunification philosophy and practice. Part 1, "Rethinking Family Reunification," suggests an approach to reunification and identifies a set of guidelines for policy, program, practice, and training. The knowledge, attitudes, and skills necessary for reunifying families are delineated in Part 2, "Family Reunification Competencies for Social Workers." Part 3, "Curriculum Modules for Teaching Family Reunification," comprises five modules on increasing competence; one module focuses extensively on child and family visiting. Part 4, "Selected References," includes references on a range of child welfare issues related to reunification.

VI. WORKING WITH THE LEGAL SYSTEM

Annotated Bibliography

Day, P., Cahn, K., & Johnson, P. (1993). Building court-agency partnerships to reunify families. In B. A. Pine, R. Warsh, & A. N. Maluccio (Eds.), *Together Again: Family reunification in foster care* (pp. 21–32). Washington, DC: Child Welfare League of America.

> The authors focus on the interagency aspects of family reunification practice, giving particular attention to the relationship among judicial personnel, legal counsel, and child welfare agency professionals. A model approach to court-agency collaboration is presented and examined for its potential and limits in improving this form of interagency practice.

Haralambie, A. M. (1993). *The child's attorney: A guide to representing children in custody, adoption, and protection cases.* Chicago: The American Bar Association.

> This book offers attorneys a step-by-step guide to preparing and trying a case. It contains advice on such topics as determining the unique needs of each child, communicating with the child, and dealing with the potential ethical conflicts between the child's best interest and his/her expressed wishes. It also contains background information on child abuse, permanency planning, and adoption. Expansive appendixes of sample forms, state statutes, and guidelines, and a table of over 250 cases and relevant state statutes are included.

Hardin, M. (Ed.). (1983). *Foster children in the courts.* Boston: Butterworth Legal Publishers.

> This well-documented book features in-depth discussion by recognized experts on an extensive range of legal issues —from emergency custody to termination of parental rights —affecting children and parents coming into contact with the court system. Chapters describe pertinent federal laws, legal processes, and implications for legal as well as social work practice.

Hardin, M. (1991). *Establishing a core of services for families subject to state intervention.* Washington, DC: American Bar Association. (Order from American Bar Association Order Fulfillment, 750 Lake Shore Drive, Chicago, IL 60611.)

> Family reunification can be delayed when parents do not receive services to address the issues that brought their children into care. State legislation often does not mandate services for children and their families beyond investigation and removal of the child when necessary. The model legislation presented in this publication addresses services in three overlapping situations: families in which a determination of abuse or neglect has been made, families with children in out-of-home care, and families whose children are the subject of child protection proceedings. Agencies and attorneys preparing legislation or regulatory or policy changes to address services will find this publication useful in identifying issues to be considered in their work.

Annotated Bibliography

Jordan, C. (1989). The Guardian ad litem: Evaluation of citizen reviewers in foster care. *Children and Youth Services Review, 11*(4), 331–348.

This study examined use of the guardian ad litem in out-of-home care reviews in a public child welfare agency. On the basis of the findings, the authors offer recommendations for effective use of external reviews by citizens.

Kaplan, S. R., & Sahonchik, K. (1993). *Overcoming barriers to permanency.* Washington, DC: American Bar Association. (Order from American Bar Association Order Fulfillment 54, 750 Lake Shore Drive, Chicago, IL 60611.)

This annotated bibliography was developed to assist child welfare agency managers, attorneys, and judges who address obstacles in their systems to permanency planning. The bibliography is divided into two sections, one management and the other legal/judicial. The authors were particularly interested in identifying locally developed training materials and studies that could be duplicated by other sites or that could serve as models for site specific work.

Katz, L. (1991). *Courtwise.* Mountlake Terrace, WA: Lutheran Social Services of Washington and Idaho. (Order from Lutheran Social Services of Washington and Idaho, 6920 220th Street, SW, Mountlake Terrace, WA 98043.)

This manual addresses the strains that social workers and legal professionals often find in their relationships with each other. Topics include basic legal principles, social work beliefs, the different approaches of the two professions, and the expertise each profession brings to case planning. The manual includes sample court orders, contracts, and written agreements.

Segal, E. C. (1988). *Evaluating and improving child welfare agency legal representation: Self-assessment instrument and commentary.* Washington, DC: ABA Center on Children and the Law. (Order from ABA Center on Children and the Law, 1800 M Street, NW, Washington, DC 20036.)

This booklet presents a tool for child welfare agencies to use in evaluating the quality of their legal representation. Areas addressed include administrative structure and operations, physical setting, staffing, and services performed. The publication includes a bibliography and is an invaluable guide for agencies and their attorneys.

Stein, T. J. (1991). *Child welfare and the law.* New York and London: Longman.

This comprehensive text takes on the special relationship between the law and social work practice in child welfare. Topics considered in depth include federal policies pertaining to the operation of child welfare programs, court decisions and client rights, reform of social service agencies through class action suits, implementation of reform measures, and participation of child welfare workers in the legal process.

VII. Funding Services and Programs

Annotated Bibliography

Center for the Study of Social Policy. *Financing family preservation: A self-assessment questionnaire.* (1993). Washington, DC: Author.

Though it was designed for family preservation in general, this helpful questionnaire can be adapted to stimulate discussion of funding for family reunification services. It provides direction in five key areas: the systems reform context, cost effectiveness, redeployment, federal fund financing and refinancing, and structural financial reform, which calls for new forms of accountability. A copy of the questionnaire can be found in the "Resources" section of this book.

Center for the Study of Social Policy. *Leveraging dollars, leveraging change: Refinancing and restructuring children's services in five sites.* Washington, DC: Author, 1991.

This report summarizes findings from the Center's work with five states and localities during 1990 and 1991. It examines how refinancing and reallocation strategies can be used to support children's services reform; presents steps to guide states in this effort; and offers an overview of what can be accomplished through commitment to revamping child and family service systems.

DeWoody, M. (1991). *Medicaid and Supplemental Security Income: Options and strategies for child welfare agencies.* Washington, DC: Child Welfare League of America.

This helpful monograph provides useful information about Medicaid and SSI. It explains the basic frameworks of these programs and how children can qualify for their benefits. It also offers strategies for using these programs to fund the provision or enhancement of health-related services to families and children.

Farrow, F. (1992). Funding initiatives for school-linked family services. In *Ensuring student success through collaboration—Summer Institute papers and recommendations of the Council of Chief State School Officers.* Washington, DC: Council of Chief State School Officers.

The author makes a strong case for the need to radically restructure and redirect entire funding streams in order for schools to make more effective supports available to the children and families who need them. The publication reviews some of the basic problems with current human service funding, discusses a framework for describing the types of funding arrangements some communities are using, and presents future steps that involve cross-system funding collaborations.

Farrow, F., & Bruner, C. (1993). *Getting to the bottom line: State and community strategies for financing comprehensive community service systems.* Falls Church, VA: National Center for Service Integration.

This monograph focuses on the concepts involved in designing new financing strategies, especially in the field of child welfare. In addition to delineating the

major principles that undergird new financing strategies, the authors review various strategies and options used by states in changing their financing systems.

Halfon, N., English, A., Allen, M., & DeWoody, M. (1994). National health care reform, Medicaid, and children in foster care. *Child Welfare, 73*, 99–115.

In the course of examining President Clinton's national health care reform proposal, the authors identify strategies for financing health care services for children in foster care through such means as innovative use of Medicaid reimbursement, provision of eligibility for supplemental benefits for all children in the child welfare system, and requiring health care providers to offer the full scope of benefits to all children in out-of-home care.

Mordock, J. B. (1989). Organizational adaptation to policy and funding shifts: The road to survival. *Child Welfare, 68*, 589–603.

This article describes a range of survival strategies employed by human service agencies in times of fiscal restraints. These include political strategies such as collaborating with other groups; funding activities such as tightening collection procedures; modification of program resources, such as simplifying the referral process; and changing structural dimensions, such as cost sharing with other agencies.

Ozawa, M. N. (1991). Basis of income support for children: A time for change. *Children and Youth Services Review, 13*(1/2), 7–27.

Based on an analysis of income supports for children, the author argues that the long-range income policy for children should emphasize society's need to invest in them through such means as children's allowances, pre- and postnatal care, medical services for all children, and refundable tax credits. These recommendations are important for family reunification services, especially in view of the impoverished status of most children and families served.

Smith, S. R. (1989). The changing politics of child welfare services: New roles for the government and the nonprofit sectors. *Child Welfare, 68*, 289–299.

The author discusses the expanding use in recent years of purchase-of-service contracts between government and nonprofit child welfare agencies for inservice to children and their families. Such use is leading to major changes in the relationship between government and nonprofit child welfare agencies, including greater government intervention and influence in nonprofit agencies.

Annotated Bibliography

Assessment, Planning, and Intervention

Children's Bureau of Los Angeles. (1991). *Family assessment form and user's guide.* Los Angeles: Author.

> This family assessment tool was developed by the Children's Bureau of Los Angeles to be used to conduct an in-home assessment of various aspects of family functioning, to develop a treatment plan, and to evaluate services. The form is completed after three home visits and the gathering of reports from others involved with the family. The *User's Guide* accompanying the tool gives clearly written, concrete examples for each topic. This makes scoring less subjective and more consistent among practitioners. Four sections assess strengths and needs in relation to the environment, caregivers, family interaction, and children. When ready to close a case, the practitioner completes the assessment a second time, thus giving the practitioner and family a concrete way to review process. The examples provided in the *User's Guide* are especially salient in that they lessen the subjectivity present in many rating scales by providing concrete guidelines for scoring.

Familystrength. (1994). *Family assessment.* Concord, NH: Author.

> This family reunification assessment and planning tool is distinctive in its focus on identifying and building on family strengths and potential, and viewing the family as partners in the reunification process. A copy may be found in the "Resources" section of this book.

Folaron, G. (1993). Preparing children for reunification. In B. A. Pine, R. Warsh, & A. N. Maluccio (Eds.), *Together again: Family reunification in foster care* (pp. 141–154). Washington, DC: Child Welfare League of America.

> The author addresses the importance of involving children throughout the reunification process, with particular attention paid to the child's developmental stage, heritage, and psychological defenses. Included are practice strategies for engaging children, assessing their commitment to reunification, helping them to communicate about the reunification effort, developing a protection plan, fostering family contact, and promoting support of foster parents.

Hess, P., & Folaron, G. (1991). Ambivalences: A challenge to permanency for children. *Child Welfare, 70,* 403–424.

> A key to determining a permanent plan for children in placement lies in understanding and working with the history and relative intensity of parental ambivalence in the parent-child relationship as it is acted out in the placement experience. This article suggests that assessing the nature and degree of a parent's ambivalence toward parenting his or her child is essential to effective child protection, placement and permanency planning services. The authors studied 40 cases of unsuccessful family reunification, examining problems

Annotated Bibliography

contributing to reunification, disruption and placement reentry, and forces contributing to and reinforcing parents' ambivalence. They recommend practice guidelines that help practitioners with questions such as the following: In which types of cases might reunification be an inappropriate initial case goal? When parents do not comply with service agreements, what steps should be taken to progress towards permanency planning for the child? When parents are not complying, when should the permanency goal be changed? After how many failed reunifications or within what time period should another case goal be established? And lastly, what should be required in terms of planning for a child before involuntary termination of parental rights is pursued? A copy of the Identifying Parental Ambivalence Worksheet may be found in the "Resources" section of this book.

Jones, M., & Biesecker, J. (1980). *Child welfare training: Goal planning in children and youth services.* Washington, DC: U.S. Department of Health and Human Services, Office of Human Development Services. Administration for Children, Youth and Families, Children's Bureau.

This training manual contains five lessons that give the reader experience in writing and developing permanent plans for children. The lessons, which include exercises, case examples, and suggestions for work with difficult clients, are designed to prepare social workers to write clear, reasonable, and measurable goals. The authors emphasize five basic goal planning steps: (1) involving the client from the beginning by initiating an assessment of the person's strengths and needs; (2) selecting reasonable, achievable goals that are meaningful to the person; (3) using the person's strengths and resources to plan the goal; (4) spelling out the steps necessary to reach each goal; and (5) documenting who will do what and when. Overall, this manual is useful for training child welfare practitioners involved in family reunification to write, implement, and evaluate case goals, with a particular emphasis on client involvement and client strengths. It would be useful to incorporate this material in a child welfare training program or as an inservice program for seasoned practitioners and agency administration.

Katz, L., & Robinson, C. (1991). Foster care drift: A risk-assessment matrix. *Child Welfare, 70,* 347–358.

This article describes a practice matrix aimed at determining the point at which delivery of maximum appropriate services to the parents will or will not bring about reunification, and when other steps to permanent placement should be taken. This matrix, which connects conditions, results, and treatment modalities, is designed for use with cases involving children age eight and under who are in out-of-home care with no relative or parent to whom they can be discharged, and who have the least chance of returning home. Parents described in this matrix need the highest number of services and the greatest intensity of service delivery to ensure permanency planning for their children. The matrix contributes to differential diagnosis of foster care cases by helping case workers toward early identification and provision of concentrated services and determination of the parents' willingness and/or ability to change. Two projects reported that workers using the matrix felt empowered to plan more aggressively for a child's permanency.

Lewis, K. (1991). A three-step plan for African American families involved with foster care: Sibling therapy, mothers' group therapy, family therapy. *Journal of Independent Social Work, 5*(3/4), 135–147.

Annotated Bibliography

The author presents a multilevel systemic treatment approach that seeks to break the cycle of entering, leaving, and reentering care, particularly in cases involving African American families. The three-step plan begins at placement and includes sibling therapy, where the children are taught to recognize their role in returning home and express their feelings in less destructive ways; mothers' group therapy, where mothers learn to feel more competent as parents and become better connected to their extended family, peer group, and community; and family therapy, where mother and children meet together to focus on issues specifically related to improving the chance of a successful reunification.

Magura, S., Moses, B. S. & Jones, M. A. (1987). *Assessing risk and measuring change in families: The Family Risk Scales.* Washington, DC: Child Welfare League of America.

This manual contains 26 standardized Family Risk Scales that identify and measure parent child and family characteristics associated with child maltreatment. The scales are used to identify children at risk for out-of-home placement in order to accurately assess and pinpoint areas where services can be provided and placement prevented. The scales can be used to monitor the effectiveness of preventive services, and facilitate the measurement of changes in risk status.

Maluccio, A. N., & Sinanoglu, P. A. (Eds). (1981). *The challenge of partnership: Working with parents of children in foster care.* New York: Child Welfare League of America.

This collection of papers on social work practice with biological parents of children in foster care examines such themes as the ecological perspective, family involvement in residential treatment, approaches to working with parents, and foster parent roles with biological parents.

Visiting

Blumenthal, K., & Weinberg, A. (1983). Issues concerning parental visiting of children in foster care. In M. Hardin (Ed.), *Foster children in the courts* (pp. 372–398). Boston: Butterworth Legal Publishers.

This chapter, aimed primarily at attorneys, discusses the importance of parent-child visiting in out-of-home care. It focuses on such areas as purpose, family issues, and the role of the agency in facilitating visits. Research on visiting has revealed that the more frequent the visiting, the more likely the child is to return home. The authors advise the reader when litigation may be necessary to encourage and enforce visiting and also provide concrete information that should be considered when formulating a visiting plan.

Hess, P. M., & Proch, K. (1993). Visiting: The heart of reunification. In B. A. Pine, R. Warsh, & A. N. Maluccio (Eds.), *Together again: Family reunification in foster care*, (pp. 119–139). Washington, DC: Child Welfare League of America.

This chapter examines the central role of visiting in achieving and maintaining family reunification. It presents the eight key purposes of visiting, offers guidelines for developing and carrying out effective visiting plans, and identifies agency resources that are essential to supporting a sound visiting program.

Hess, P. M., & Proch, K. O. (1988). *Family visiting in out-of-home care: A guide to practice.* Washington, DC: Child Welfare League of America.

This publication can help practitioners develop visiting plans that facilitate achievement of case goals and thus decrease the length of time children spend in out-of-home care. It discusses the purpose of visiting and the agency sup-

Annotated Bibliography

ports that optimize visiting, casts visiting as an essential component of agency service, and provides guidelines for developing visiting plans that consider the strengths and limitations of the children, family of origin, and foster family. Included are specific and useful suggestions for preparing participants for visits and for evaluating and documenting visits. A discussion of ways in which staff can manage their own stress related to planning and carrying out visits is also included

Simms, M. D., & Bolden, B. J. (1991). The Family Reunification Project: Facilitating regular contact among foster children, biological families, and foster families. *Child Welfare, 70,* 679–690.

This article describes a 16-week pilot program aimed at enhancing the prospects for reunification through a carefully planned visiting and support program. In addition to providing structured parent-child visits, the project included support and training for foster parents and a support group for biological parents. The effort was successful in creating a supportive and neutral environment for visiting in order to achieve case goals. The project also increased cooperation between mental health care providers and child welfare practitioners in their work with families separated by placement. A major finding was the need to extend the period of support beyond the 16-week period for a number of families experiencing multiple problems.

Residential Facilities

Carlo, P., & Shennum, W. (1989). Family reunification efforts that work: A three year follow-up study of children in residential treatment. *Child and Adolescent Social Work, 6,* 211–216.

A three-year follow-up study of children discharged from a residential treatment program was conducted to determine the long-term family reunification rates. Of primary interest was a comparison of families that had received different types of parent involvement programs during their child's placement. The study showed that the program that combined experiential learning (contact between parent and child) and didactic learning (systematic instruction) proved to be the most effective. Seventy-eight percent of the families involved in the "combined experiential/didactic" modality remained reunited at the three-year mark, as compared to 27% of the "separate experiential or didactic" families at follow-up.

Falk, R. (1990). Family reunification in a residential facility. *Residential Treatment for Children & Youth, 7*(3), 39–49.

This article describes the addition of a family reunification program to an existing treatment program for adjudicated delinquent adolescent boys. Families are invited to live in an apartment located on the grounds of the institution and to participate in family therapy sessions, allowing for on-the-spot observation of family dynamics and appropriate intervention. The agency offers family services as one of several programs to the young clients in order to satisfy their contract with the placing agency, which often identifies the adolescent as the sole client and focus of treatment. Although the results are tentative, the program seems to be effective in reducing runaway behavior and program failures. Additionally, it appears to have been successful in reuniting youngsters with their families. By providing a milieu for parents to experiment with living together as a family with their estranged youngster, family members can be reassured in a relatively safe environment. Families learn to communicate more

204

© 1996 CHILD WELFARE LEAGUE OF AMERICA

effectively, to approve of and accept one another, to play together, and to simply enjoy each other's company. Such a program not only facilitates a youth's return home but also provides the family with alternative and productive ways to stay together.

Annotated Bibliography

Gibson, D., & Noble, D. (1991). Creative permanency planning: Residential services for families. *Child Welfare, 70*, 371–382.

The authors describe a creative program for single mothers and their families in which a children's facility provides residential service for the entire family. Over several months, the staff (who reside with their own families on campus with the clients' families) provide direct services that include role modeling and "on-the-job training" for mothers in the enhancement of family relationships; appropriate child guidance and discipline procedures; effective communication skills; emotional and physical nurturance techniques, including handling grief and stress and planning leisure activities; preparing nutritious affordable meals; providing supportive bedtime procedures; assisting children in school study; planning for meeting future needs of their families; and creating a healthy life-style for themselves, such as making time for exercise, personal development, and relationships. Aftercare services are provided for a minimum of six months after discharge from the program. Overall, the program approach has been cost effective as well as effective in keeping families together. Of the 46 families (with a total of 86 children) served between 1986 and 1988, only two families were later separated by a child's out-of-home placement.

206

PART 5

RESOURCES

SUMMARY

This section contains selected guidelines and forms to help you make needed improvements in your family reunification services. These resources are organized into the following sections:

I. Enhancing Cultural Competence

II. Funding Services and Programs

III. Working with Children and Families

I. Enhancing Cultural Competence

Criteria for Assessing and Selecting Appropriate
Foster Family Placements for Children of
Mixed African American and Caucasian Parentage*

Resources

Child

- Does the child have a preference regarding the race(s) of foster parents?

- With what race(s) does the child currently identify?

Child's Family

- Do the child's parents have a preference regarding race(s) of foster parents?

- Who will be visiting the child—family, friends, others—and will they be comfortable visiting in the potential family foster home?

Potential Foster Family Placement

- What are the foster parents' motivations for choosing to foster children who have both African American and Caucasian parents?

- What is the racial background of the foster family members and of other foster children in the home?

- What are the foster parents' general attitudes and opinions about persons of African American and Caucasian parentage, African Americans, and Caucasians?

- How do the foster parents view children of mixed parentage in terms of racial identity?

- How do the foster parents' extended family and social network view children of African American and Caucasian parentage and the children's parents?

- How often do the foster parents have social contacts with members of different races? What is the nature of those contacts and the level of satisfaction they yield?

- Are the foster parents knowledgeable about or do they have access to knowledge about proper care of the child's skin, hair, and diet?

- What are the foster parents' feelings regarding visiting in their home? Would the child's family members or the child's friends of any race be welcome?

- Is there literature in the home endorsed by members of the child's cultures and heritages?

- Would the foster parents enable their foster child to attend the church of the child's family's choice?

---

* Excerpted with permission of the authors. From Folaron, G., & Hess, P. M. (1993). Placement considerations for children of mixed African American and Caucasian parentage, *Child Welfare*, 72, 113-125.

Resources

Community Environment of Potential Foster Family

- What is the racial makeup of the foster parents' neighborhood and school district?

- Will the child be accepted by the neighbors, school, religious organization, and foster parents' employers?

- Do perceptions of school personnel in the foster parents' school district support or block a positive racial identity in children of mixed parentage?

Financing Family Preservation:
A Self-Assessment Questionnaire*

Resources

A. Introduction

Family preservation services (FPS)can be an effective means to prevent unnecessary placement in out-of-home care, while keeping children safely in their own homes. When properly designed, delivered, and targeted, FPS can also reduce, or slow the growth of, out-of-home care caseloads and costs. We have learned a great deal in the last ten years about how to plan for, implement, and finance FPS.

The following "self-assessment" questionnaire is intended to help state and local officials structure a discussion of the status of their service and financial planning for FPS. The questionnaire starts with the system reform context within which FPS planning must be done and progresses through a systematic review of key issues and financing approaches for FPS and related services. The questionnaire can be used to help construct a program, financial, and political action plan to advance FPS as part of a larger reform effort for family and children services.

Many of the questions posed in the questionnaire are difficult and will not be easily answered in a single session. The best approach may be to take a first cut at all of the questions, and then return to those which require more discussion and follow-up. The questions can also be used to focus work on financing strategies when state teams return home.

B. The Systems Reform Context

Family preservation services are an important part—but just one part—of the larger movement to reform family and children services and improve outcomes for children. Options for financing FPS make more sense when long-term goals for FPS are clearly framed within a larger strategic plan.

1. *FPS Program and Fiscal Goals:* Have you established clear program and financial goals for FPS? Do you know what your system would look like if you could serve all "appropriate" families? (See question C1 below.)

2. *Combined Program and Fiscal Strategy:* Where do plans for FPS fit in the larger cross-systems reform efforts of your state? Have you developed a multi-year program and fiscal strategy which moves the family and children service system away from crisis-oriented categorical programs, toward more prevention-oriented, community-based systems of care?

---

* Prepared by the Center for the Study of Social Policy, 1250 Eye Street, NW, Washington, D.C. 20005 (December 1993). Reprinted by permission of the Center for the Study of Social Policy.

C. Cost Effectiveness

FPS is financial viable because, when properly planned and implemented, it can save or avoid [the spending of] more money than it costs. The cost effectiveness of FPS hinges on two factors: first, the accuracy of targeting FPS to families whose children would enter care without help, and second, the effectiveness of the service model in preventing out-of-home placement for those families. Note that service effectiveness is not the same as the "success rate" commonly quoted for FPS programs. All programs collect information on the overall success rate (i.e., the percent of children in families served who did not enter out-of-home care.) This overall rate can be misleading because it increases when the wrong families are served by the program (i.e., those whose children would not have entered care anyway.) The relevant success rate, but one more difficult to establish, is the success rate for properly targeted families at imminent risk of out-of-home placement.

1. *Targeting Accuracy:* Do you know the rate at which you are serving the "right" families? Do you have a good operational definition of "imminent risk of placement"? Do you have the capacity to analyze the way placement decisions are actually made in your state and develop (or refine) your approach to targeting? Have you considered plans to use FPS models for reunification services targeted to children already in out-of-home care?

2. *Service Effectiveness:* Do you know the rate at which your FPS model prevents (delays, shortens, or lessens) the usage of out-of-home care for families at imminent risk of placement?

3. *Cost-Benefit Analysis:* Have you completed a cost-benefit analysis of your FPS program—either through formal evaluation, or self-evaluation tracking and reporting (or both)?

D. Redeployment

Redeployment means using the money we already have—and should always be the financing option of first choice. FPS can often be financed through redeployment of funds in the out-of-home care budget. This approach to financing builds on the cost-benefit analyses discussed above. It depends on well-developed consensus forecasts of what caseloads will be without an investment in family preservation services. And it requires an understanding of how and when to use cost-avoidance and cost-savings arguments in the state's budget and political processes. Using redeployment, FPS can be, at least partially, self-financing within a one- to two-year budget cycle.

1. *Consensus Forecast of Out-of-Home Care:* Have you developed a long-range (minimum three year) forecast of out-of-home care caseloads and cost? Do you have a process by which to establish broad-based (executive and legislative) consensus on such forecasts?

2. *Return on Investment Analysis:* Have you completed a financial analysis which estimates the return on investment by fiscal year from new expenditures on FPS?

3. *Budgetary Redeployment:* Have you used such consensus forecasts and return on investment analyses to justify the transfer of state general funds from out-of-home care to FPS (and/or Reunification)?

E. Federal Fund Financing and Refinancing

There are now well-established models for using federal funds for family preservation. The most important of these models are those which use two of the remaining uncapped federal titles: Title IV-A Emergency Assistance and Title XIX Medicaid. The federal matching rate under Title IV-A for all states is 50%. For Medicaid, the federal match ranges from 50% to about 80%. In some states with high Medicaid federal matching rates (above 60%) these fund sources are used in tandem, with FPS charged first to Medicaid for Medicaid-eligible families, and to Title IV-A for all other families.

By using federal funds to pay for FPS, the general fund cost of FPS is reduced, and the net cost benefit of the service is increased. Where states have established large FPS programs with 100% state and local funding, these federal titles can be used to refinance existing Family Preservation Services. The proceeds of this effort can then be reinvested and rematched to pay for significant expansion of FPS. Federal fund financing and refinancing efforts are administratively complex, and always require an upfront investment in infrastructure (staff, systems, etc.) to assure that federal claims are correctly prepared and do not result in later audit disallowance and repayment.

The greatest danger in federal fund refinancing efforts is that the freed-up money will be used for deficit reduction or some other purpose not related to improved family and children's services. The best way to prevent this is to have a compelling program agenda ready to finance, and to orchestrate the discussion of refinancing revenues so that they can be clearly linked to this agenda. In some states, the governor or legislature has established commitments by executive order or legislation to reinvest funds generated by refinancing into improved family and children services.

Finally, the Family Preservation and Family Support Act included in OBRA '93 provides a small but important new resource to build FPS and Family Support programs. This money will have little effect if it is used to cover the costs of normal growth in these programs or is spread thin across many programs and providers. States should use the new funds strategically to expand services for families and support new approaches to service delivery. States should also work to stretch these funds as far as possible by matching them with other fund sources. One interesting approach being considered is a method which allows some new IV-B funds to be effectively matched with IV-A funds. After states have decided what portion of the new funds to use for family support, they may use some or all of the remaining portion to replace existing general funds used for family support. The freed-up general funds can then be used to expand FPS, with 50% matching under Title IV-A. This approach will meet maintenance of effort requirements since combined expenditures for family preservation and family support will increase in accord with federal requirements.

1. *IV-A and Medicaid:* Are you using IV-A and/or Medicaid to pay for FPS? Are there specific obstacles or questions you need answered to help move these financing approaches forward?

2. *The New IV-B Funds:* How does your state plan to use this money strategically? Do you know how to effectively match some of the new IV-B funds with Title IV-A?

3. *Reinvestment:* Does your state have a commitment from the governor or legislature to reinvest the proceeds of federal fund refinancing efforts into

Resources

FPS or other services for families and children? If not, do you have a politically sound plan to get such a commitment?

F. Structural Financial Reform

The current system of services for families and children is built on narrowly defined categories, with financial incentives skewed in the direction of placement in out-of-home care. Unless financial structures and incentives are changed, it is possible that the system will revert to old behavior, once the impetus for reform has passed.

The current system uses categories of children and categories of service to ration care and hold agencies accountable for narrowly authorized use of funds. Some states are developing new forms of accountability, which replace narrow categories with more broadly based responsibility for achieving outcomes for children. Under these systems, the old categories of federal funding (Titles IV-E, and Medicaid) are not eliminated, but moved to the "back room" of a seamless service system which offers families and children what they need in the "front room." Within this approach, duplicative service structures can be combined and resources pooled. The growth of such service and the systems which govern them is an evolutionary process which takes time to fully develop.

1. *Cross-Systems Gatekeeping and FPS:* Do your state financial structures support the ability of local cross-systems collaboratives to purchase or administer common functions like intake, assessment, and family preservation?

2. *Incentives:* Do your financial systems provide incentives to preserve families? Which is easier for caseworkers: putting children in foster care, or supporting the family so that the child may remain safely at home? Do communities get to keep a portion of the caseload savings associated with preventing growth in out-of-home care?

3. *Seamless Service Systems, Fund Pools, and New Forms of Accountability:* What are you doing to help communities develop seamless service systems and new forms of accountability for using dollars to get results?

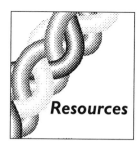

Identifying Parental Ambivalence Worksheet*

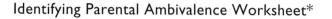

The purpose of this worksheet is to organize information from a child's placement history that may indicate patterns of a parent and/or a child's feelings and behaviors that reflect deeply felt or persistent ambivalence about the parent-child relationship. Exploration and assessment of the nature and degree of ambivalence related to this relationship is essential to effective child protection, placement, and permanency planning services. Assessment includes not only accurate identification of parents' and children's verbal and behavioral indicators of ambivalence, but also exploration to assure correct interpretation of the meaning of statements and behaviors. Selection of a realistic permanent plan involves determining: 1) whether the parents are able or can become able to meet a minimum sufficient level of care for an individual child; 2) whether the parent is willing to do what is necessary to be able to meet this level of care and to do so within a period of time fair to the child; and 3) where the child feels he or she belongs.

Child: _____

Parent A: _____

Parent B: _____

In the boxes below, write A and/or B as it applies in each space. For example, if parent A voluntarily placed the child for the first placement, put an A in the voluntary space under placement 1.

1.

Placements	1	2	3	4
Voluntary	___	___	___	___
Involuntary	___	___	___	___

* Developed by Peg Hess, PhD, ACSW, and Gail Folaron, MSW, ACSW, for the Professional Review Action Group Project, 1990. PRAG is a collaborative project between the Indiana State Department of Public Welfare, District VII, and the Indiana University School of Social Work, supported by funds granted by the U.S. Department of Health and Human Services, Office of Human Development Services, Administration for Children, Youth and Families, Award #90-CWC948. Reprinted by permission of the authors.

2.

Did parent A/B...	Placements		1	2	3	4
consistently visit? .... Yes	No		___	___	___	___
consistently participate in court? .... Yes	No		___	___	___	___
consistently participate in services? ..... Yes	No		___	___	___	___
refuse any service? .... Yes	No		___	___	___	___
(name of service _____)						

3. During any period of time did the parent refuse to visit or postpone visiting with the child? If so, which child, for what reasons, and for how long a time period?

Parent A: _____

Parent B: _____

4. Did either parent ever suggest the child might be better off in an adoptive home, long-term foster care, or guardian placement?

Parent A: _____

Parent B: _____

5. During any placements did the parent request that a child's return home be postponed and placement extended? If so, which parent/child, for what reason, and for how long?

Placement 1: _____

Placement 2: _____

Placement 3: _____

Placement 4: _____

6. Has parent ever planned to relinquish custody of this child or any other child? If so, which child and did parent follow through? What type of custodial agreement was considered (e.g., adoption, guardianship)?

Parent A: _____

Parent B: _____

7. Did parent make extensive or inappropriate use of respite care or other form of child relief while child was in the home?

Parent A: _____

Parent B: _____

8. Are there comments in the record or otherwise known about what parents said regarding parenting this child?

Parent A: _____

Parent B: _____

9. Are there comments in the record or otherwise known about child's preference in living situation?

    _____

    _____

10. Are there observations from foster parents, relatives, community service providers or in written evaluations or reports regarding child/parent attitude about reunification? If so, what?

    Child: _____

    Parent A: _____

    Parent B: _____

11. What is your gut feeling about child/parent attitude regarding reunification?

    Child: _____

    Parent A: _____

    Parent B: _____

218

Working with Children and Families

Familystrength Family Assessment*

Resources

Family: _____ Intake Date: _____

Presenting Issue/Reason for Referral (family & collateral):

Brief History (timeline, frequency, related events, previous efforts at solutions, use of other services, recent changes): _____
_____
_____
_____

Present Situation and Desired Outcome (3 or more views):

	Family	Collateral	Familystrength
Placement Potential/Re-unification Plan: What has to happen for child to stay/return home?			
Current Issue(s): What are you most concerned about now?			
Recent Successes: What changes and exceptions have already happened/been accomplished?			
Outcome criteria: How will you know/what will it look like when the reunification is stable? What will be happening instead?			

* Developed by Familystrength, Concord, NH. (1994). Reprinted with permission.

Resources

Current Family Situation (family, household composition; basic physical and safety needs; areas of success/independence; employment, income, and education [only if relevant to placement issues]):

_____

_____

Tracking/Current Status of Presenting Issue (tracking of problem and exceptions, i.e., when problem is not occurring):

family description of frequency, duration of problem:

_____

_____

collateral description (school, placement, foster home) of interactions:

_____

_____

observation during assessment:

_____

_____

Family Interactional Patterns Related to Issue and Solutions (family members' behavior/interaction during exception [when problem isn't occurring]; past successful family problem-solving; approaches to teaching discipline; structures and routines; communication):

_____

_____

_____

Social and Community Relationships (informal support system, extended family, family relationship with school, helping relationships):

_____

_____

_____

Skill Assessment/Strengths (how family has solved problem before; family's ideas/ attempts at solutions; how family members learn new things):

_____

_____

_____

Goals; Outcome Criteria (necessary events/outcomes for child to return/stay at home; family members strengths/abilities to ensure successful reunification):

_____

_____

_____

WORKING WITH CHILDREN AND FAMILIES

Development of Safety Plans in Reunification Cases*

Resources

by Peg McCartt Hess, Gail Folaron, & Ann Jefferson

A safety plan is a written agreement between the family and agency/ professionals for the purpose of protecting the children from further abuse or neglect and eliminating the need for further placement. The following issues should be addressed in safety plans prepared as part of the service process and included in treatment and legal records.

- What was the original family need/problem(s) and how has it been resolved?

- What is required of the parent(s) and other family members to prevent recurrence of the problem? If relevant, what is required of the child(ren) to prevent recurrence of the problem? Include specific behaviors which either must or must not occur.

- Following reunification, what are the warning signs that abuse/neglect may occur? (For example, parent resumes drinking, perpetrator visits home, parents stop medication.)

- If warning signs occur, what specific steps will be taken and by whom?

- What options are available to the parents if the parents experience difficulty?

- What specific conditions or circumstances would result in reentry?

- Following reunification, who will see the parents? How often? How will the agency responsible for child protection receive feedback?

- Following reunification, who will see the child(ren)? How often? How will the agency responsible for child protection receive feedback?

- Following reunification, what agreements are in place with respect to services available to family members and with respect to requirements for service use? What level of participation is expected?

- Following reunification, what household conditions (i.e., locks on doors) or specific household risks (i.e., pets or unsanitary conditions) must be repaired, eliminated, or controlled to assure the child's safety?

- Following reunification, what is the responsible agency's plan for monitoring the family's and service providers' adherence to service agreements? Who will notify the responsible agency if service plans are not adhered to? Is there a plan to assure needed community services to the family beyond child protective agency case closure?

- What would be the case goal if the child(ren) reenters placement? (reunification, emancipation, guardianship, termination of parental rights for adoption, other).

* From materials developed for use in the Marion County Department of Public Welfare (Indianapolis, IN), 1990, through a collaborative project between the Indiana State Department of Public Welfare, District VII, and the Indiana University School of Social Work, funded in part by the U.S. Department of Health and Human Services, Administration for Children, Youth, and Families, Grant # 90-CW0948. Reprinted with permission.

Resources

Family Protection Plan:
Outline for Discussion with Family*

by Peg McCartt Hess, Gail Folaron, & Ann Jefferson

When abused/neglected children and their families provided with services in their own homes or when families are preparing for either unsupervised visits during placement or reunification following placement, the family and professionals serving the family must develop a family protection or safety plan—a written agreement between the family and agency/professionals for the purpose of protecting the children from further abuse or neglect. Discussion including all family members is important to ensure that everyone understands the plan and can identify warning signs and to ensure that family members are able to carry out the plan if warning signs do appear or family members feel at risk. Discussion of areas in addition to those outlined below may be relevant depending on each family's circumstances. Professionals serving the family should assure that the safety plan is reviewed periodically and revised as needed.

Family

- What are the family's plans for preventing further abuse/neglect (e.g., involvement in specific services, use of alternative methods of discipline, plans for privacy, etc.)?

- What are the warning signs that abuse/neglect may recur?

- Are there persons with whom family members are to have no contact?

- Are there persons with whom the child(ren) is(are) to have supervised visits only?

- What is the plan if agreements/court orders regarding no contact/supervised visits are violated?

- What is the specific concrete plan for the family if warning signs or abuse/neglect occur (i.e., respite, support groups, services available, whom to call, where to go, placement, etc.)?

Child

- Depending on age and capacity, what are the child(ren)'s plans for self-protection if warning signs or if abuse/neglect reoccurs? Is the child able to identify and describe warning signs?

* Adapted from materials developed for use in the Marion County Department of Public Welfare (Indianapolis, IN), 1990, through a collaborative project between the Indiana State Department of Public Welfare, District VII, and the Indiana University School of Social Work, funded in part by the U.S. Department of Health and Human Services, Administration for Children, Youth and Families, Grant #90-CW0948. Reprinted with permission.

Resources

- Does the child have the information and skills necessary to implement the plan? (For example, can the child identify people to call? Can the child get to a phone? Does the child know how to dial the phone? Does the child know the phone number?)

Parent(s)

- What are the parent(s)' plans for self/child protection if there are warning signs or if abuse/neglect reoccurs?

- Has the parent(s) explained the plan to the children?

- Has the parent given children permission to carry out the plan? (Parents should give children permission in the presence of professionals during the planning process.)

- Do parents have a supportive network (other than professionals) to help out when there is a problem (e.g., neighbors, extended family, friends, church members)?

Other Family Members

- What are the other family members' plans for self/child protection if there are warning signs that occur or if abuse/neglect reoccurs?

Professionals

- What roles/responsibilities have all professionals (health care, social services, others) involved with the family agreed to? Who will actually see the child(ren) and monitor their care and safety?

224

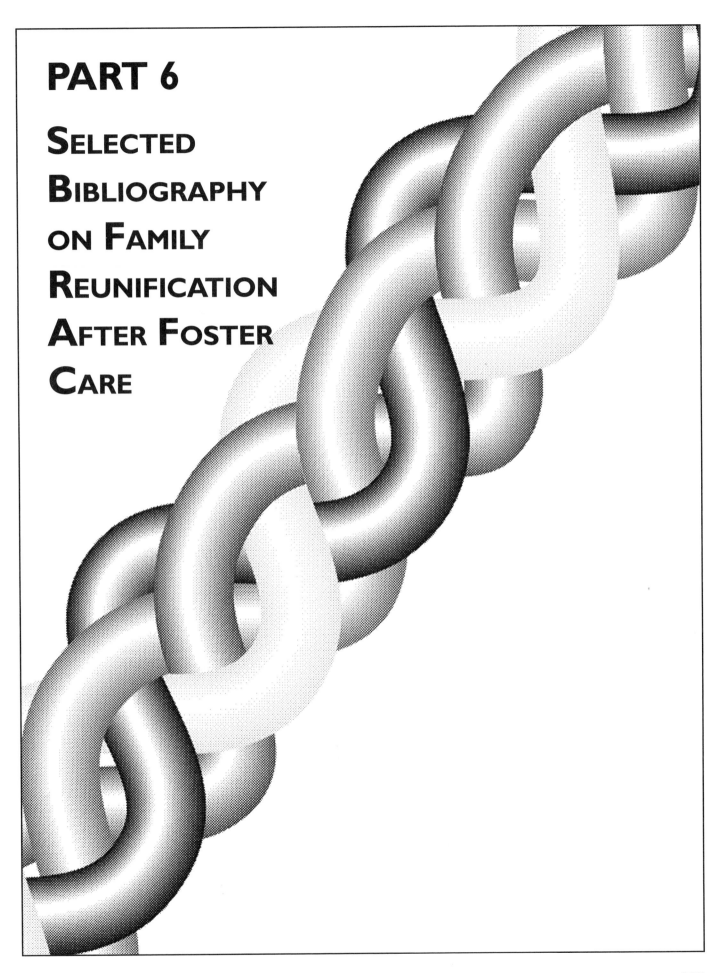

PART 6

SELECTED BIBLIOGRAPHY ON FAMILY REUNIFICATION AFTER FOSTER CARE

Abramczyk, L. W., & Ross, J. W. (Eds.). (1993). *International reunification symposium.* Columbia, SC: University of South Carolina College of Social Work.

Aldgate, J., Pratt, R., & Duggan, M. (1989). Using care away from home to prevent family breakdown. *Adoption and Fostering, 13*(2), 32–37.

Aldgate, J., Maluccio, A., & Reeves, C. (1989). *Adolescents in foster families.* London: B. T. Batsford, and Chicago: Lyceum Books.

Barth, R. P., & Berry, M. (1987). Outcomes of child welfare services under permanency planning. *Social Service Review, 61,* 71–90.

Beckerman, A. (1989). Incarcerated mothers and their children in foster care: The dilemmas of visitation. *Children and Youth Services Review, 11,* 175–183.

Benedict, M. I., & White, R. B. (1991). Factors associated with foster care length of stay. *Child Welfare, 70,* 45–58.

Benedict, M., White, R. B., & Stallings, R. (1987). Race and length of stay in foster care. *Social Work Research and Abstracts, 23*(4), 23–26.

Berrick, J. D., Barth, R. P., & Needell, B. (1994). A comparison of kinship foster homes and foster family homes: Implications for kinship foster care as family preservation. *Children and Youth Services Review, 16*(1/2), 33–63.

Berry, M. (1988). A review of parent training programs in child welfare. *Social Service Review, 62,* 302–323.

Block, N. M. (1981). Toward reducing recidivism in foster care. *Child Welfare, 60,* 597–610.

Blumenthal, K., & Weinberg, A. (1983). Issues concerning parental visiting of children in foster care. In M. Hardin (Ed.), *Foster children in the courts* (pp. 372–398). Boston: Butterworth Legal Publishers.

Blumenthal, K., & Weinberg, A. (Eds.). (1984). *Establishing parent involvement in foster care agencies.* New York: Child Welfare League of America.

Brown, C. L., & Little, S. (1990). Family reunification. *Children Today, 19*(6), 20–23, 33.

Bryce, M., & Lloyd, J. C. (Eds.). (1981). *Treating families in the home—An alternative to placement.* Springfield, IL: Charles C Thomas.

Bullock, R., Little, M., & Millham, S. (1993). *Going home—The return of children separated from their families.* Aldershot, England, and Brookfield, VT: Dartmouth Publishing Co.

Cahn, K., & Johnson, P. (Eds.). (1993). *Children can't wait: Reducing delays for children in out-of-home care.* Washington, DC: Child Welfare League of America.

Selected Bibliography

Carlo, P., & Shennum, W. A. (1989). Family reunification efforts that work: A three year follow-up study of children in residential treatment. *Child and Adolescent Social Work, 6,* 211–216.

Carlo, P. (1985). The children's residential treatment center as a living laboratory for family members: A review of the literature and its implications for practice. *Child Care Quarterly, 14,* 156–170.

Carlo, P. (1988). Implementing a parent involvement/parent education program in a children's residential treatment center. *Child and Youth Care Quarterly, 17,* 195–206.

Carlo, P. (1993). Parent education vs. parent involvement: Which type of efforts work best to reunify families? *Journal of Social Service Research, 17,* 135–150.

Child Welfare League of America. (1990). *Standards for services to strengthen and preserve families with children.* Washington, DC: Author.

Edna McConnell Clark Foundation. (1985). *Keeping families together: The case for family preservation.* New York: Author.

Cole, E., & Duva, J. (1990). *Family preservation: An orientation for administrators and practitioners.* Washington, DC: Child Welfare League of America.

Courtney, M. F. (1994). Factors associated with the reunification of children and their families. *Social Service Review, 68,* 82–108.

Davis, I. P., & Ellis-MacLeod, E. (in press). Temporary foster care: Separating and reunifying families. In J. Blacher (Ed.), *When there is no place like home.* Baltimore: Paul H. Brooks Publisher.

Davis, I.P., English, D. J., & Landsverk, J. A. (1993). *Going home—and returning to care: A study of foster care reunification.* San Diego, CA: San Diego State University, College of Health and Human Services, School of Social Work, and the Child and Family Research Group.

Falk, R. (1990). Family reunification in a residential facility. *Residential Treatment for Children and Youth 7*(3), 39–49.

Fanshel, D., Finch, S. J., & Grundy, J. F. (1990). *Foster children in a life course perspective.* New York: Columbia University Press.

Fanshel, D., & Shinn, E. B. (1978). *Children in foster care—A longitudinal investigation.* New York: Columbia University Press.

Fein, E., & Maluccio, A. N. (1984). Children leaving foster care: Outcomes of permanency planning. *Child Abuse and Neglect 8,* 425–431.

Fein, E., Maluccio, A. N., Hamilton, V. J., & Ward, D. (1983). After foster care: Outcomes of permanency planning for children. *Child Welfare, 62,* 485–558.

Fein, E., Maluccio, A. N., & Kluger, M. (1990). *No more partings: An examination of long-term foster family care.* Washington, DC: Child Welfare League of America.

Fein, E., & Staff, I. (1993). Findings from a reunification services program. *Child Welfare, 62,* 25–40.

Fein, E., & Staff, I. (1991). Implementing reunification services. *Families in Society, 72,* 335–343.

Festinger, T. (1994). *Returning to care: Discharge and reentry into foster care.* Washington, DC: Child Welfare League of America.

Finch, S., Fanshel, D., & Grundy, J. (1986). Factors associated with the discharge of children from foster care. *Social Work Research and Abstracts, 22*(1), 10–18.

Selected Bibliography

Gibson, T. L., Tracy, G. S., & DeBord, M. S. (1984). An analysis of the variables affecting length of stay in foster care. *Children and Youth Services Review, 6*, 135–145.

Goerge, R. M. (1990). The reunification process in substitute care. *Social Service Review, 64*, 422–457.

Hardin, M. (Ed.). (1983). *Foster children in the courts*. Boston: Butterworth Legal Publishers.

Hess, P. M., & Folaron, G. (1991). Ambivalences: A challenge to permanency for children. *Child Welfare, 70*, 403–424.

Hess, P. M., & Proch, K. (1986). How the states regulate parent-child visiting. *Public Welfare, 44*(4), 12–17.

Hess, P. M., & Proch, K. O. (1988). *Family visiting in out-of-home care: A guide to practice*. Washington, DC: Child Welfare League of America.

Jorejsi, C. R., Bertsche, A. V., & Clark, F. W. (1981). *Social work practice with parents of children in foster care—A handbook*. Springfield, IL: Charles C Thomas.

Hubbell, R., Hirsch, G., Barrett, B., Condelli, L., & Plantz, M. (1986). *Evaluation of reunification for minority children*. Washington, DC: CSR, Inc.

Jenkins, S., Diamond, B. E., Flanzraich, M., Gibson, J. W., Hendricks, J., & Marshood, N. (1983). Ethnic differential in foster care placements. *Social Work Research and Abstracts, 19*(4), 41–45.

Jones, M. A. (1985). *A second chance for families: Five years later*. New York: Child Welfare League of America.

Kadushin, A., & Martin, J. A. (1988). *Child welfare services* (4th ed.). New York: Macmillan Publishing Co.

Kagan, R., & Schlosberg, S. (1989). *Families in perpetual crisis*. New York: W.W. Norton.

Kaplan, L. (1986). *Working with multi-problem families*. Lexington, MA: Lexington Books.

Kelsall, J., & McCullough, B. (1988). *Family work in residential child care: Partnership in practice*. Cheadle, England: Boys' and Girls' Welfare Society.

Knitzer, J., & Yelton, S. (1990). Collaborations between child welfare and mental health. *Public Welfare, 48*(2), 24–33.

Lloyd, J. C., & Bryce, M. E. (1984). *Placement prevention and family reunification: A handbook for the family-centered practitioner* (rev.). Iowa City, IA: National Resource Center on Family Based Services, The University of Iowa School of Social Work.

Maluccio, A. N., Fein, E., & Davis, I. P. (1994). Family reunification: Research findings, issues, and directions. *Child Welfare, 73*, 489–504.

Maluccio, A. N., Fein, E., & Olmstead, K. A. (1986). *Permanency planning for children: Concepts and methods*. London and New York: Routledge, Chapman, and Hall.

Maluccio, A. N., Krieger, R., & Pine, B. A. (1991). Preserving families through family reunification. In E. M. Tracy, D. A. Haapala, J. Kinney, & P. J. Pecora (Eds.), *Intensive family preservation services: An instructional sourcebook* (pp. 215–235). Cleveland, OH: Case Western Reserve University, Mandel School of Applied Social Services.

Maluccio, A. N., Pine, B. A., & Warsh, R. (1994). Protecting children by preserving their families. *Children and Youth Services Review, 16*, 295–307.

Selected Bibliography

Maluccio, A. N., & Sinanoglu, P. A. (Eds.). (1981). *The challenge of partnership: Working with parents of children in foster care.* New York: Child Welfare League of America.

Maluccio, A. N., Warsh, R., & Pine, B. A. (1993). Rethinking family reunification after foster care. *Community Alternatives—International Journal of Family Care, 5*(2), 1–17.

Maluccio, A. N., & Whittaker, J. K. (1988). Helping the biological families of children in out-of-home placement. In E. W. Nunally, C. S. Chilman, & F. M. Cox (Eds.), *Troubled relationships* (pp. 205–217). Newbury Park, CA: Sage Publications.

Marsh, P., & Triseliotis, J. (Eds.) (1993). *Prevention and rerunification in child care.* London: B. T. Batsford Ltd.

Maybanks, S., & Bryce, M. E. (Eds.). (1979). *Home-based services for children and families: Policy, practice, and research.* Springfield, IL: Charles C Thomas.

McGowan, B. G., & Meezan, W. (Eds.). (1983). *Child welfare: Current dilemmas—Future directions.* Itasca, IL: F.E. Peacock Publishers.

McMurtry, S., & Young Lie, G. (1992). Differential exit rates of minority children in foster care. *Social Work Research and Abstracts, 28*(1), 42–48.

Mech, E. V. (1985). Parental visiting and foster placement. *Child Welfare, 64,* 67–72.

Millham, S., Bullock, R., Hosie, K., & Haak, M. (1986). *Children lost in care: The family contact of children in care.* Farnborough, England: Gower.

Millham, S., Bullock, R., Hosie, K., & Haak, M. (1986). *Lost in care: The problems of maintaining links between children in care and their families.* Aldershot, England: Gower.

Olsen, L. (1982). Services for minority children in out-of-home care. *Social Service Review, 56,* 572–585.

Oyserman, D. & Benbenishty, R. (1992). Keeping in touch: Ecological factors related to foster care visitation. *Child and Adolescent Social Work Journal, 9,* 541–554.

Pike, V., Downs, S., Emlen, A., Downs, G., & Cae, D. (1977). *Permanent planning for children in foster care: A handbook for social workers.* Washington, DC: U.S. Department of Health, Education, and Welfare, Publication No. (OHDS) 78–30124.

Pine, B. A., Warsh, R., & Maluccio, A. N. (Eds.). (1993). *Together again: Family reunification in foster care.* Washington, DC: Child Welfare League of America.

Ratterman, D. (1990). Detrimental to the best interests of the child: When the agency's failure to make diligent efforts or allow visitation can be excused in a termination action. *Children's Legal Rights Journal, 11*(2), 2–7.

Rosenberg, L.A. (1991). Psychological factors in separation and reunification: The needs of the child and of the family. *Children's Legal Rights Journal, 12*(1), 20–24.

Rowe, J., Cain, H., Hundleby, M., & Keane, A. (1984). *Long-term foster care.* London: Batsford/British Agencies for Adoption and Fostering.

Rowe, J., Hundleby, M., & Garnett, L. (1989). *Child care now—A survey of placement patterns.* London: British Agencies for Adoption and Fostering.

Rzepnicki, T. L. (1987). Recidivism of foster children returned to their own homes: A review and new directions for research. *Social Service Review, 61,* 56–70.

Seaberg, J. R., & Tolley, E. S. (1986). Predictors of length of stay in foster care. *Social Work Research and Abstracts 22*(3), 11–17.

Simms, M. D., & Bolden, B. J. (1991). The family reunification project: Facilitating regular contact among foster children, biological families, and foster families. *Child Welfare, 70*, 679–690.

Sinanoglu, P. A., & Maluccio, A. N. (Eds.). (1991). *Parents of children in placement: Perspectives and programs.* Washington, DC: Child Welfare League of America.

Staff, I., & Fein, E. (1994). Inside the black box: An exploration of service delivery in a family reunification program. *Child Welfare, 73*, 195–211.

Stein, T. J. (1991). *Child welfare and the law.* New York: Longman.

Stein, T. J., Gambrill, E. D., & Wiltse, K. T. (1978). *Children in placement: Perspectives and programs.* New York: Praeger Publishers.

Stein, T. J., & Rzepnicki, T. L. (1983). *Decision making at child welfare intake.* New York: Child Welfare League of America.

Teare, J. F., Furst, D. W., Peterson, R. W., & Authier, K. A. (1992). Family reunification following shelter placement: Child, family and program correlates. *American Journal of Orthopsychiatry, 62*, 142–146.

Thoburn, J. (1990). *Success and failure in permanent family placement.* Aldershot, England: Gower Publishing Co.

Triseliotis, J. (Ed.). (1980). *New developments in foster care and adoption.* London: Routledge and Kegan Paul.

Turner, J. (1984). Reuniting children in care with their biological parents. *Social Work, 29*, 501–505.

Turner, J. (1984). Predictors of recidivism in foster care: Exploratory models. *Social Work Research and Abstracts, 20*(2), 15–20.

Walton, E. (1991). *The reunification of children with their families: A test of intensive family treatment following out-of-home placement* (unpublished doctoral dissertation, Graduate School of Social Work, University of Utah).

Walton, E., Fraser, M. W., Lewis, R. E., Pecora, P. J., & Walton, W. K. (1993). In-home family-focused reunification: An experimental study. *Child Welfare, 72*, 473–487.

Warsh, R., Maluccio, A. N., & Pine, B. A. (1994). *Teaching family reunification: A sourcebook.* Washington, DC: Child Welfare League of America.

Werrbach, G. B. (1993). The family reunification role-play. *Child Welfare, 72*, 555–568.

Whittaker, J. K., Kinney, J., Tracy, E., & Booth, C. (Eds.). (1990). *Reaching high-risk families: Intensive family preservation in the human services.* Hawthorne, NY: Aldine de Gruyter.

Wulczyn, F. (1991). Caseload dynamics and foster care reentry. *Social Service Review, 65*, 133–156.

Yosikikami, R., et al. (1983). *Assessing the implementation of federal policy to reduce the risk of foster care: Placement prevention and reunification in child welfare.* Portland, OR: Regional Research Institute for Human Services, Portland State University.

232

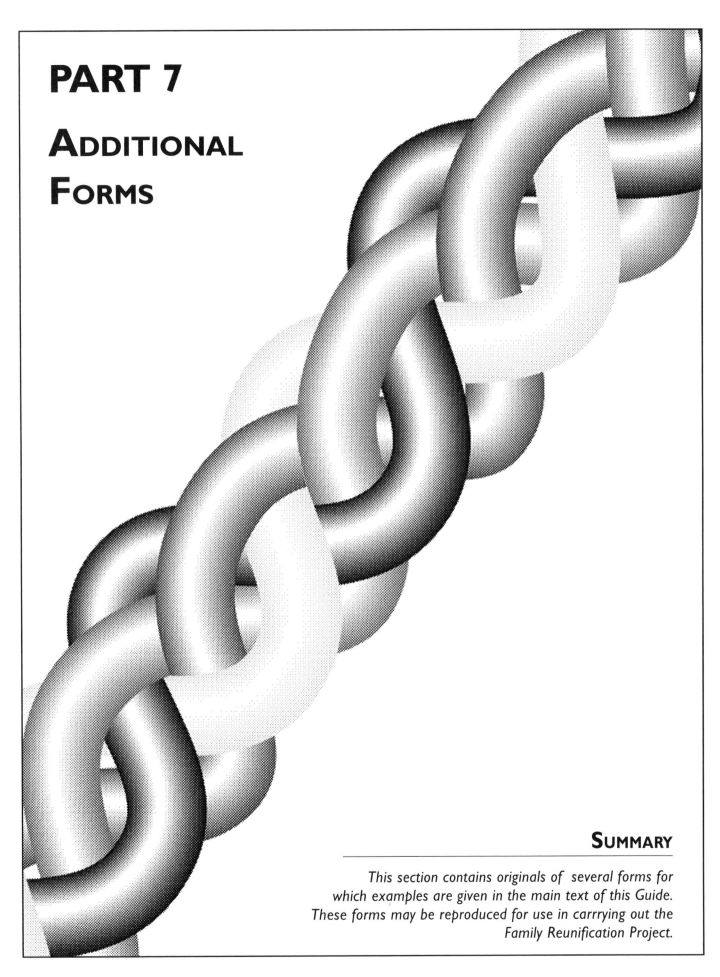

PART 7

ADDITIONAL
FORMS

SUMMARY

This section contains originals of several forms for which examples are given in the main text of this Guide. These forms may be reproduced for use in carrrying out the Family Reunification Project.

234

Summary of Work Team Recommendations

Component #: _____

Policy Recommendations

_____
_____
_____
_____
_____
_____
_____
_____

Training Recommendations

_____
_____
_____
_____
_____
_____
_____

Resource Recommendations

_____
_____
_____
_____
_____
_____

Principle A

With its emphasis on ensuring continuity of relationships and care for children, family reunification is an integral part of the philosophy of permanency planning.

In order to accomplish this, we recommend that:

_____

_____

_____

_____

_____

_____

_____

_____

_____

_____

_____

_____

_____

_____

_____

_____

_____

_____

_____

_____

_____

_____

_____

_____

Principle B

Children are best reared in families, preferably their own; most families can care for their own children if properly assisted.

In order to accomplish this, we recommend that:

_____

_____

_____

_____

_____

_____

_____

_____

_____

_____

_____

_____

_____

_____

_____

_____

_____

_____

_____

_____

_____

_____

_____

_____

_____

Principle C

Family reunification practice must be guided by an ecologically oriented, competence-centered perspective that emphasizes promoting family empowerment; engaging in advocacy and social action; reaching for—and building on—family strengths; involving any and all whom the child considers family as partners; and providing needed services and supports.

In order to accomplish this, we recommend that:

_____

_____

_____

_____

_____

_____

_____

_____

_____

_____

_____

_____

_____

_____

_____

_____

_____

_____

_____

_____

_____

_____

_____

_____

_____

Principle D

Teamwork among the many parties involved in family reunification is critical.

In order to accomplish this, we recommend that:

_____

_____

_____

_____

_____

_____

_____

_____

_____

_____

_____

_____

_____

_____

_____

_____

_____

_____

_____

_____

_____

_____

_____

_____

_____

_____

Principle E

All forms of human diversity — cultural, racial, ethnic, religious, life-style—as well as physical and mental challenges, must be respected.

In order to accomplish this, we recommend that:

_____

_____

_____

_____

_____

_____

_____

_____

_____

_____

_____

_____

_____

_____

_____

_____

_____

_____

_____

_____

_____

_____

_____

_____

_____

_____

_____

Principle F

A commitment to early and consistent child-family visiting is an essential ingredient in preparing for—and maintaining—reunification.

In order to accomplish this, we recommend that:

_____

_____

_____

_____

_____

_____

_____

_____

_____

_____

_____

_____

_____

_____

_____

_____

_____

_____

_____

_____

_____

_____

_____

_____

_____

_____

_____

_____

241

Principle G

Foster parents and child care workers must be involved as members of the service delivery team. The agency should share information with them about the child and family that is shared with other service providers, involve them in decisions, and provide them with adequate training.

In order to accomplish this, we recommend that:

_____

_____

_____

_____

_____

_____

_____

_____

_____

_____

_____

_____

_____

_____

_____

_____

_____

_____

_____

_____

_____

_____

_____

_____

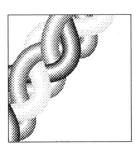

Principle H

Many families will have continuing service needs in multiple areas. Services to meet these needs must be provided for as long as children and families require them to maintain the reunification.

In order to accomplish this, we recommend that:

_____

_____

_____

_____

_____

_____

_____

_____

_____

_____

_____

_____

_____

_____

_____

_____

_____

_____

_____

_____

_____

_____

_____

_____

_____

243

Principle J

Agencies must empower their staffs by providing adequate training and supervision and by using a team approach in making case decisions.

In order to accomplish this, we recommend that:

_____

_____

_____

_____

_____

_____

_____

_____

_____

_____

_____

_____

_____

_____

_____

_____

_____

_____

_____

_____

_____

_____

_____

_____

_____

_____

_____

_____

_____

FAMILY REUNIFICATION

An Expanded Definition

Family reunification is the planned process of reconnecting children in out-of-home care with their families by means of a variety of services and supports to the children, their families, and their foster parents or other service providers. It aims to help each child and family to achieve and maintain, at any given time, their optimal level of reconnection—from full reentry of the child into the family system to other forms of contact, such as visiting, that affirm the child's membership in the family.

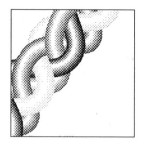

A. With its emphasis on ensuring continuity of relationships and care for children, family reunification is an integral part of the philosophy of permanency planning.

B. Children are best reared in families, preferably their own; most families can care for their own children if properly assisted.

C. Family reunification practice must be guided by an ecologically oriented, competence-centered perspective, that emphasizes:

- promoting family empowerment;

- engaging in advocacy and social action;

- reaching for—and building on—family strengths;

- involving any and all whom the child considers family as partners; and

- providing needed services and supports.

D. Teamwork among the many parties involved in family reunification is critical.

E. All forms of human diversity—ethnic, racial, cultural, religious, life-style—as well as physical and mental challenges, must be respected.

F. A commitment to early and consistent child-family visiting is an essential ingredient in preparing for—and maintaining—reunification.

G. Foster parents and child care workers must be involved as members of the service delivery team. The agency should share information with them about the child and family that is shared with other service providers, involve them in decisions, and provide them with adequate training.

H. Many families will have continuing service needs in multiple areas. Services to meet these needs must be provided for as long as children and families require them to maintain the reunification.

I. Agencies must empower their staffs by providing adequate training and supervision and by using a team approach in making case decisions.

The Components of Family Reunification

The Agency

1. Mission and Principles
2. Financial Management
3. The Work Environment
4. Workloads
5. Recruitment
6. Cultural Competence
7. Social Worker Roles and Responsibilities
8. Foster Parent Roles and Responsibilities
9. Supervision
10. Staff Development
11. Program Monitoring and Evaluation

Family Reunification

12. Assessment and Goal Planning
13. Preparing Families for Reunification
14. Preparing Children for Reunification
15. Visiting
16. Postreunification Services

Interorganizational Relations

17. Funding Sources
18. Governmental Bodies
19. External Reviewers
20. Cross-System Collaboration
21. Court and Legal Systems
22. Community Provider Agencies
23. Law Enforcement Agencies
24. School Systems
25. Public Relations and Information

Visiting is the heart of all plans to reunify families. It helps maintain family ties as well as provide opportunities for family members to learn and practice new behaviors and styles of communicating. Agencies should provide and support quality visiting services that promote a child's timely return home or make possible a determination that he/she cannot return to full-time care in the family. Whether or not children are able to return home, visiting maintains family ties that are essential to a child's healthy development.*

Key Elements for Success...

A. Agencies place children near their parents and other significant family members.

B. Agencies place siblings together unless otherwise indicated.

C. Visiting environments make use, whenever possible, of natural settings, such as parks, zoos, children's museums, and the like.

D. The agency encourages foster parents to allow family visits in the foster home, unless contraindicated.

E. The agency has well-equipped, comfortable visiting rooms.

F. The agency provides flextime or compensatory time for workers so that visits can occur when families can schedule them.

G. The agency makes available to foster and biological families financial assistance for such visit-related expenses as transportation or food.

H. Staff and foster parents receive training in planning and carrying out positive visits.

I. The agency requires written visiting plans that specify visit purposes, frequency, length, location, supervision, participants, supportive services, and planned activities.

J. Children, family, foster parents, and staff participate in decisions about visiting.

K. Visiting plans balance the child's need for protection with the family's need for autonomy.

continued...

---

* P. M. Hess & K. O. Proch, *Family visiting in out-of-home care: A guide to practice* (Washington, DC: Child Welfare League of America, 1988).

L. Visit activities are chosen by the social worker and the family that provide both children and families with opportunities to learn, practice and demonstrate new behaviors and patterns of interaction.

M. The social worker adequately prepares children, families, and foster parents for visits and gives them opportunities to work through their reactions to visits.

N. The practitioner arranges visits along a continuum of increasingly stressful times (e.g., playing in the park to mealtimes to difficult bedtimes) to help families gradually achieve competence in these areas.

O. The practitioner evaluates, alters, and documents the visiting plan in accordance with family and child progress and needs.

P. Visits are used to assess realistically whether family members have made the changes necessary to decrease the risks to the child in the home.

Q. Children are returned home only after they have safely had unsupervised visits in their own home, including overnight visits and visits lasting several days or more, over an appropriate period of time.

This activity involves small groups of members of all of the Family Reunification Project teams, as well as invited guests, working together to turn the recommendations of the Work Team into a beginning set of action plans for the agency. The main purposes of the exercise are to:

- clarify the issues and concerns (and personal experiences) discussed in the Work Team meetings that led to the recommendation;

- provide an opportunity for agency staff members to consider how they might contribute to making the recommended change in the service delivery system, whether that contribution is at the policy level, administrative level, or practice level; and

- implement an action planning process that will result in a plan to address at least one recommendation in each small group.

The activity is conducted in two parts. Part I (one hour) focuses on each group's discussion of the recommendations under one of the principles that form the framework for the Work Team Final Report. By the conclusion of Part I, each group will select one recommendation to work on during the afternoon session, based on the following criteria:

- The agency could feasibly plan and accomplish some action steps to achieve the recommendation within the next six months to a year.

- The action plan for addressing the recommendation would make the most use of the potential contributions of the members of the small group.

- Implementing of the recommendation would make a significant contribution to improving the agency's ability as an agency to reconnect families.

In Part II, the small groups develop and prepare to present an action plan (90 minutes). Each small group then reports out to the group as a whole (30 minutes).

Use this planning tool to turn each of the recommendations of the Work Team into a set of action plans for the agency.

Principle:____

_____
_____
_____
_____

Work Team Recommendation

_____
_____
_____
_____

Key Issues Related to This Recommendation

(i.e., What is the rationale for this recommendation? What examples from your practice support this needed change? What additional comments or questions do you have about it?)

_____
_____
_____
_____
_____
_____
_____
_____
_____
_____
_____
_____
_____
_____
_____
_____
_____

Action Steps Needed:

_____
_____
_____
_____
_____
_____
_____
_____
_____
_____
_____

Resources and Supports Needed for Implementation:

(i.e., what obstacles must be overcome, and what resources are needed to carry out the action steps successfully in such areas as space, personnel, time, money, and sanctions?)

_____
_____
_____
_____
_____
_____
_____

Measures of Success (in six months):

_____
_____
_____
_____
_____
_____
_____
_____

Measures of Success (in one year):

_____
_____
_____
_____
_____
_____
_____
_____
_____

PLANNING FOR CHANGE MEETING EVALUATION

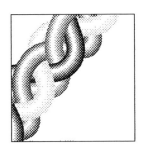

The overall purposes of this meeting are to examine the results of the self-assessment of our family reunification services and begin to create an action plan for system change.

To what extent did the following aspects of the meeting help or hinder achieving these purposes?

- the introductory sessions:

  _____
  _____
  _____

- the small group exercise:

  _____
  _____
  _____

- the mix of participants:

  _____
  _____
  _____

- the written materials:

  _____
  _____
  _____

- the facility:

  _____
  _____
  _____

- other:

  _____
  _____
  _____

253

CERTIFICATE OF APPRECIATION

extends its deep appreciation to

for participating in the

FAMILY REUNIFICATION PROJECT

APPENDIX
THE RESOURCE WORKBOOK

Assembling the Resource Workbook

Resource Workbook Materials

256

ASSEMBLING THE RESOURCE WORKBOOK

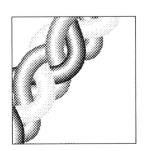

All team members should be provided with a copy of the *Reconnecting Families Resource Workbook* at the Orientation Meeting. You may photocopy from the *Guide* the materials that comprise the *Resource Workbook,* using the instructions below, or you may purchase bound copies using the form at the end of the *Guide.*

Directions

Each *Resource Workbook* should contain copies of the following pages. Numbers on the pages should be changed before reproduction to reflect the true pagination of the *Resource Workbook.*

1. Title page (see page 259).

2. Copyright notice (see page 260)—Although permission is granted to reproduce the indicated pages for the *Resource Workbook,* the Child Welfare League of America maintains ownership of all the materials. These materials may not be reproduced for any purpose other than use in the Family Reunification Project.

3. Contents (see page 261-262)—Page numbers should be added to the contents page to reflect the final pagination of the *Resource Workbook.*

4. Preface (see pages 263–264).

5. Introduction (see pages 265–266).

6. Components and Key Elements for Success (see pages 69–70 and pages 73-180)—Substitute pages 267-268 for pages 71-72. Additionally, block out the words "Part 3" from page 69 before photocopying.

7. Annotated Bibliography (see pages 181–206)—Block out the words "Part 4" from page 181 before photocopying.

8. Resources (see pages 207–224)—Block out the words "Part 5" from page 207 before photocopying.

9. Selected Bibliography on Family Reunification After Foster Care (see pages 225–232)—Block out the words "Part 6" from page 225 before photocopying.

10. About the Authors (see page 269).

   Don't forget to renumber the pages before photocopying.

RECONNECTING FAMILIES

A GUIDE TO STRENGTHENING FAMILY REUNIFICATION SERVICES

RESOURCE WORKBOOK

Robin Warsh

Barbara A. Pine

Anthony N. Maluccio

CWLA PRESS • WASHINGTON, DC

CWLA Press is an imprint of the Child Welfare League of America.

© 1996 by the Child Welfare League of America, Inc. All rights reserved. Neither this book nor any part may be reproduced or transmitted in any form or by any means, electronic or mechanical, including photocopying, microfilming, and recording, or by any information storage and retrieval system, without permission in writing from the publisher.

For information on this or other CWLA publications, contact the CWLA Publications Department at the address below.

CHILD WELFARE LEAGUE OF AMERICA, INC.
440 First Street, NW, Suite 310, Washington, DC 20001-2085

CURRENT PRINTING (last digit)
10 9 8 7 6 5 4 3 2 1

Cover and text design by Jennifer R. Geanakos

Printed in the United States of America

ISBN # 0-87868-640-1

CONTENTS

Contents

> "If we keep thinking we're doing it right, we're never going to improve."
>
> —*A Social Worker*

Contents

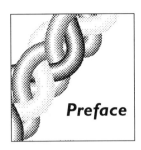

Whether or not to reunite children in out-of-home care with their families of origin is one of the most complicated decisions that child welfare practitioners face. Difficult questions loom: How do we *both* preserve families and protect children from harm? What constitutes "good enough" parenting? How do we weigh the risk of returning children to their families against the risk of prolonging their stay in family foster care? Moreover, once the reunification decision has been made by all involved, how do we implement it well?

In response to these questions, public as well as private child welfare agencies have been reexamining their family reunification policies and services. Accordingly, *Reconnecting Families: A Guide to Strengthening Family Reunification Services,* and this *Resource Workbook* are designed to help you conduct a comprehensive self-assessment of the policies, programs, practices, and resources your agency has in place to help reunify children in out-of-home care with their families. The Family Reunification Project, as we have termed this self-assessment, will also help you to evaluate your agency's relationships with other parts of the service delivery system, particularly the courts, community provider agencies, and schools. When completed, the assessment will produce a full picture of the strengths and limitations of all the components of your family reunification service delivery system, as well as a plan for improving it.

The above-mentioned *Guide* and this *Resource Workbook* are the outcome of a two-year grant we received in 1992 from The Annie E. Casey Foundation to develop, field test, refine, and publish a self-study manual to help agencies evaluate and strengthen their family reunification service delivery systems. By the end of the first year we had developed a draft of the assessment tool and a preliminary set of resource materials. Still needed, however, was a method for agencies to use in carrying out the assessment and change process.

Convinced that system change must occur from the bottom up, as well as from the top down, we created an approach that involved staff members at all levels of the agency who, through group discussion and decision making, would be able to examine their own practice and agency supports and recommend improvements. To see if the approach worked, we turned to the Connecticut Department of Children and Families (DCF) to conduct a comprehensive field test of the *Guide.* During the spring and summer of 1993, we observed the DCF staff as they used the *Guide,* asking questions and refining the assessment process. This experience taught us a sound method for conducting the assessment that is firmly grounded in the reality of child welfare practice today.

We are indebted to DCF for agreeing to serve as the site of the field test of *Reconnecting Families.* Throughout the experience, DCF held fast to its commitment to the philosophy of family preservation, to the value of self-assessment leading to system change, and to the provision of needed resources in order that our work could be carried out.

> There seemed to be a special closeness of people gathered for a common purpose—to create a better system to help families. It was refreshing to have my input valued. I believe real good will come from this effort.
>
> —*A Work Team Member*

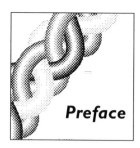

Preface

In addition to DCF staff, we have had the good fortune of working with many supporters of and national experts on family reunification, each of whom provided invaluable guidance on the development of this publication. These persons are named in the *Guide;* their large number attests to the spirit of collaboration and range of perspectives that gave shape and meaning to this volume. We are grateful to them and welcome the opportunity to continue to work with this group of forward-thinking and creative professionals in other efforts to bring about improved child welfare service delivery.

As we learned during the field test, the *Guide* is a powerful tool for unleashing creativity and teamwork among staff members. The process of self-assessment and change that the *Guide* calls for conveys a new approach to shaping a responsive child welfare system, one that is shared by staff members at all levels. We hope that the Family Reunification Project will prove useful to you in examining and strengthening the range of services your agency provides to children and their families. We welcome the opportunity to hear about your experiences with it.

It was a rare and rewarding opportunity to think about where we want the department to go. . . to get advice and insights from the staff who work with children and families every day . . . and to use their recommendations to plan and carry out needed improvements. It was great to be a part of such positive change.

—A Work Team Member

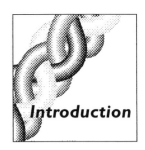
Although comprehensive national data are not available, most children in out-of-home care do return home. In 1990, 67% of the 202,000 children who left out-of-home care were either reunited with their families or placed with relatives.* Large numbers of those who return home, however, eventually reenter care. Wulcyzn ** found a 22% reentry rate for children reunited with their families in New York State, and Goerge† reported a 33% reentry rate for families reunited in Illinois. These numbers were a major force behind our work on *Reconnecting Families: A Guide to Strengthening Family Reunification Services*, as they suggest an urgent need to improve services that help families to reconnect and remain together.

The *Guide* contains all of the materials needed to undertake the self-assessment, with the exception of copies of various publications and resources that are recommended. It is designed to prepare your Project Coordinator to lead you through the self-assessment process and develop plans for improved service delivery. The self-assessment is based on a "Framework for Assessment of Strengths and Needs." This consists of 25 system components of an agency's service delivery system. They are organized in three sections that correspond with the three major contexts of the system: the child welfare agency as an organization, its family reunification services, and its relationship with other key organizations and systems. The list of all 25 components may be found on the contents pages as well as in the section of this *Resource Workbook* on "Introduction to the Framework and Components."

This *Resource Workbook* contains each of these components, which are briefly defined and followed by a set of "Key Elements for Success," representing standards of best practice. A set of worksheets is also included; your Project Coordinator will provide instructions for using these. Additionally, in preparation for taking part in the assessment, you will be asked to read *Together Again: Family Reunification in Foster Care.* We have also included an annotated bibliography that relates to selected components in the Framework; a selection of resources to help you make needed improvements in your family reunification services, and a selected bibliography on family reunification after foster care.

Benefits of Participating in the Self-Assessment

For a number of reasons, the self-assessment process that underpins the project is as important as the results it produces. First, as a tool for self-assessment, the

> I am grateful for the opportunity to discuss and share ideas for bringing about more effective ways to serve our children and families. The process was enlightening for the whole team.
>
> —A Work Team Member

---

* T. Tatara, *Characteristics of children in substitute and adoptive care: A statistical summary of the VCIS National Child Welfare Data Base—Based on FY 82 through FY 90 data* (Washington, DC: American Public Welfare Association, 1993).

** F. Wulczyn, Caseload dynamics and foster care reentry, *Social Service Review*, 65 (1991): 133–156.

† R. M. Goerge, The reunification process in substitute care, *Social Service Review*, 64 (1990): 422–457.

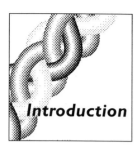

Introduction

Family Reunification Project calls for an open discussion of agency strengths and needs by the staff members who actually plan and carry out the family reunification work. This is no audit by outside experts, no judgment by people who do not walk in your shoes.

Second, the Family Reunification Project is carried out by staff members from all levels of the agency—including policymakers, managers, supervisors, trainers, social workers, foster parents, attorneys, staff members from community agencies—as well as by biological parents. The project brings together the full range of players involved in family reunification work to consider current practices and problems. The process of shared problem-solving can result in a "we're in this together" attitude, as people at all levels in the system are reminded of how complex family reunification work is, how difficult it is to create and maintain a responsive child welfare system, and how every person plays a vital part in shaping services.

Third, the Family Reunification Project is a teaching tool. Because we have been working together for over eight years and with others around the country to develop family reunification materials, *Reconnecting Families: A Guide to Strengthening Family Reunification Services* contains information on the current best thinking about family reunification policy and practice. Participants in the assessment process thus gain exposure to a wealth of practice strategies and approaches.

Fourth, in field testing, participants received a tremendous morale and creativity boost. Involvement in the assessment and planning process provides staff members and others with the opportunity to reflect on their work and consider, in lively exchanges with their coworkers, new and better ways to meet the needs of families. The process also produces a sense of optimism that improvements can, in fact, be made. Optimistic and empowered staff members are better able to foster these qualities in the families they serve.

Finally, the Family Reunification Project's model of self-assessment and planning for system change in family reunification featured here is one that can be adapted to evaluate other programs and services in your agency.

Introduction to the Framework and Components

The Framework for Assessment of Strengths and Needs consists of 25 components organized within the three major contexts of the family reunification system: The Agency (the child welfare agency as an organization), Family Reunification Services (the agency's family reunification services), and Interorganizational Relations (the agency's relationship to other organizations and systems).

In this *Resource Workbook*, each component is briefly described, followed by a set of Key Elements for Success that reflect best practice in that particular area. You will be helped to think about the Key Elements by reading chapters from *Together Again: Family Reunification in Foster Care*. Worksheets are also provided to help you conduct the assessment.

The Components of Family Reunification

The first 11 components of family reunification relate to your agency's organizational structure: its purposes, personnel, and procedures. Attention to these key elements helps strengthen administrative capability. Components 12 to 16 address family reunification practice issues. Assessment and action planning in this area will result in more responsive direct services to children and their families. The final nine components focus on your agency's relationship with the "outside world." Improvements here enhance your agency's capacity to be a full member of the larger system of care.

> The process was empowering. We had the opportunity to share our experiences, learn from each other, and collectively develop a vision of possibilities for our children and families.
>
> —*A Work Team Member*

I. The Agency

1. Mission and Principles
2. Financial Management
3. The Work Environment
4. Workloads
5. Recruitment
6. Cultural Competence
7. Social Worker Roles and Responsibilities
8. Foster Parent Roles and Responsibilities
9. Supervision
10. Staff Development
11. Program Monitoring and Evaluation

II. Family Reunification Services

12. Assessment and Goal Planning
13. Preparing Families for Reunification
14. Preparing Children for Reunification
15. Visiting
16. Postreunification Services

III. Interorganizational Relations

17. Funding Sources
18. Governmental Bodies
19. External Reviewers
20. Cross-System Collaboration
21. Court and Legal Systems
22. Community Provider Agencies
23. Law Enforcement Agencies
24. School Systems
25. Public Relations and Information

ABOUT THE AUTHORS

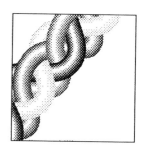

Robin Warsh was the Director of "Preserving Families Through Reunification," a system reform project,* of which this publication is one outcome. She is a Lecturer at Boston College Graduate School of Social Work, teaches and writes on family preservation, and provides consultation to public and private child welfare agencies.

Barbara A. Pine was the Senior Consultant for "Preserving Families Through Reunification." She is Professor of Social Work at the University of Connecticut; teaches and writes on child welfare policy and practice, ethics, and social work administration; and provides consultation to public and private child welfare agencies.

Anthony N. Maluccio was the Principal Investigator for "Preserving Families Through Reunification." He is Professor of Social Work and Chair of the Doctoral Program at Boston College Graduate School of Social Work. He teaches and writes extensively on family and children's services, clinical social work, and social work research methods.

* Funded by The Annie E. Casey Foundation (1992–1993), grant # 92–1300.

TEACHING FAMILY REUNIFICATION

A SOURCEBOOK

Robin Warsh, Anthony N. Maluccio, Barbara A. Pine

The Child Welfare League of America • Washington, DC

This *Sourcebook*, by the authors of *Together Again* and *Reconnecting Families*, provides an important set of resources for training and educating child welfare and social service workers for the challenge of managing family reunification. Each curriculum may be used by itself or in conjunction with broader inservice training or education.

Contents: Rethinking Family Reunification: Guidelines for Policy, Program, Practice, and Training; Family Reunification Competencies for Social Workers; Curriculum Models for Teaching Family Reunification: Redefining Family Reunification, Differing Perspectives on Family Reunification, Developing Policy and Program in Family Reunification, Visiting—The Heart of Reunification, Learning from a Case Study; Handouts; and Bibliography.

TO ORDER:

CWLA c/o CSSC
P.O. Box 7816
300 Raritan Center Parkway
Edison, NJ 08818
800/407–6273
908/225–1900
Fax 908/417–0482

Please specify stock #5111. CWLA pays shipping and handling for prepaid U.S. orders. Bulk discount policy (not for resale): 10–49 copies, 15%; 50 or more copies, 20%. Canadian and foreign orders must be prepaid in U.S. funds. MasterCard/Visa accepted.

1994/0-87868-511-1/#5111 $24.95

Use this form to order:

TOGETHER AGAIN
FAMILY REUNIFICATION IN FOSTER CARE

and

RECONNECTING FAMILIES
RESOURCE WORKBOOK

YES! Please send me:

_____ copies of *Together Again* at $21.95 (stock #5251)

_____ copies of *Resource Workbook* at $9.95 (stock #6401)

Call or Fax for Priority Service!
Call 800/407–6273 or 908/225–1900 Monday-Friday during regular business hours (ET) or Fax 908/417–0482 anytime.

(Please type or print clearly)

Name _____

Organization _____

Address _____

City _____ State_____ Zip_____-_____

Daytime telephone: (_____) _____

Money-Saving Payment Option
CWLA pays shipping and handling for prepaid U.S. orders. Bulk discount policy (not for resale): 10–49 copies, 15%; 50 or more copies, 20%. Canadian and foreign orders must be prepaid in U.S. funds by international money order.

☐ Check enclosed, payable to CWLA.

Other Payment Options (Charge my)

☐ MasterCard   ☐ Visa

Acct.# _____

Exp.Date _____

_____
Print name as it appears on card

_____
Signature

P.O. attached. # _____

Child Welfare League of America
c/o CSSC
300 Raritan Center Parkway
P.O. Box 7816
Edison, NJ 08818–7816

Use this form to order:

TOGETHER AGAIN
FAMILY REUNIFICATION IN FOSTER CARE

and

RECONNECTING FAMILIES
RESOURCE WORKBOOK

YES! Please send me:

_____ copies of *Together Again* at $21.95 (stock #5251)

_____ copies of *Resource Workbook* at $9.95 (stock #6401)

Call or Fax for Priority Service!
Call 800/407–6273 or 908/225–1900 Monday-Friday during regular business hours (ET) or Fax 908/417–0482 anytime.

(Please type or print clearly)

Name _____

Organization _____

Address _____

City _____ State_____ Zip_____-_____

Daytime telephone: (_____) _____

Money-Saving Payment Option
CWLA pays shipping and handling for prepaid U.S. orders. Bulk discount policy (not for resale): 10–49 copies, 15%; 50 or more copies, 20%. Canadian and foreign orders must be prepaid in U.S. funds by international money order.

☐ Check enclosed, payable to CWLA.

Other Payment Options (Charge my)

☐ MasterCard   ☐ Visa

Acct.# _____

Exp.Date _____

_____
Print name as it appears on card

_____
Signature

P.O. attached. # _____

Child Welfare League of America
c/o CSSC
300 Raritan Center Parkway
P.O. Box 7816
Edison, NJ 08818–7816

Use this form to order:

TOGETHER AGAIN
FAMILY REUNIFICATION IN FOSTER CARE

and

RECONNECTING FAMILIES
RESOURCE WORKBOOK

YES! Please send me:

_____ copies of *Together Again* at $21.95 (stock #5251)

_____ copies of *Resource Workbook* at $9.95 (stock #6401)

Call or Fax for Priority Service!
Call 800/407–6273 or 908/225–1900 Monday-Friday during regular business hours (ET) or Fax 908/417–0482 anytime.

(Please type or print clearly)

Name _____

Organization _____

Address _____

City _____ State_____ Zip_____-_____

Daytime telephone: (_____) _____

Money-Saving Payment Option
CWLA pays shipping and handling for prepaid U.S. orders. Bulk discount policy (not for resale): 10–49 copies, 15%; 50 or more copies, 20%. Canadian and foreign orders must be prepaid in U.S. funds by international money order.

☐ Check enclosed, payable to CWLA.

Other Payment Options (Charge my)

☐ MasterCard   ☐ Visa

Acct.# _____

Exp.Date _____

_____
Print name as it appears on card

_____
Signature

P.O. attached. # _____

Child Welfare League of America
c/o CSSC
300 Raritan Center Parkway
P.O. Box 7816
Edison, NJ 08818–7816

272